KB202087

The Feasibility of a Korea-China FTA and its Potential Economic Effects

한국-중국의 실현 가능한
FTA와 잠재적 경제효과

The Feasibility of
a Korea-China FTA
and its Potential Economic Effects

한국－중국의 실현 가능한
FTA와 잠재적 경제효과

| Zhao Jin long

ABSTRACT

This dissertation examines the feasibility and effects of the China-Korea free trade agreement(CK FTA) in various sectors of the two countries' economies using a general equilibrium model and incorporating the most recent Global Trade Analysis Project Database. Above all, both China and Korea's FTA strategies together with their respective FTA motives are elaborated, given by the demonstration and analysis of two countries' trade features, trade structures and bilateral investment. According to the analysis on Korea and China's trade relations, the industrial advantages and disadvantages between the two countries are matched against the Revealed Comparative Advantage index and Intra-Industry Trade index.

Following the model's aggregations, two scenarios are devised so as to evaluate the potential economic impacts of China-Korea FTA. Results from a partial albeit more realistic FTA scenario have been compared to the maximum potential economic effects expected by a full free trade agreement. It comes as no surprise that the agreement gains are shown to be higher, as more barriers to trade are removed. Hence, the economic benefits are expected to be greater for a full trade agreement while relatively smaller in the realistic partial trade agreement. In details, the changes in the two countries' welfare, GDP, Trade, Economic Output by sector in the full scenario are greater than their counterpart in the partial one, either in relative or absolute terms. The simulation results simplify that the effects of CK FTA are closely relevant to the scenario constructions and the industrial gains in the two countries are unevenly distributed. Korea would witness much more expansion in its manufacture sectors while China is expected to increase more in its food sectors, basically because China's manufactures are more protected through import tariffs than Korea's. On the other hand, Korean agriculture initially is more protected from international competition than China's.

The welfare system of Korea and China would both profit from two scenarios projected by simulation results. Korea would enjoy relatively greater returns in welfare. Korea's obvious reliance on trade with China and comparatively higher existing tariffs in its agriculture sector may explain its potential for welfare increase. Trade effects on two countries' exports and imports are presented in percentage change and volume term, exploring the changes from different aspects. The results indicate smaller import and export changes for China but larger import and export changes for Korea in relative change. However, two countries' import and export changes in absolute volume are quite close, which explains the different original trade volumes in the base year.

This study also suggests import and export increases for main economic sectors both in China and Korea. As to the bilateral trade balance, Global Trade Analysis Project (GTAP) model simulations confirm that either Korea or China's trade balance will become worse although the absolute volumes are not strong enough in both scenarios. While output *on average* would increase in both economies, on the industrial level, some industries in both economies will expand while others are expected to contract. In general, as could be expected, the domestic industries with higher ex-ante levels of import protection are those expected to decrease as a result of increased trade and competition. With regards to expected changes in sector output, a pattern emerges where there is a drop in many manufactures for China, while the output for many agricultural sectors will increase.

The advantageous situation for Korea's industry, featuring strong competition, will expand while rice and other crops are expected to contract as a result of lacking international competition. However, the overall picture for evaluating FTA prospects is more complex. In a realistic scenario, according to the simulation resluts, Korean Textiles, Apparel and leather will see the largest increase in production, while the largest decrease is found in the sectors for rice and other food. It should be noted that the agricultural sector enjoys high a priori import protection. Therefore, the removal of tariffs means that an FTA will have a strong impact on Korean agriculture. For China, a mirroring pattern is predicted: the relatively largest decline is found in the textiles, apparel and leather. The largest increases in output for China are found in other crops where China's ex-ante trade barriers were much lower than it Korean counterparts.

The demand changes for labor and capital are exposed in the final part of this thesis, which reflects the flow of the primary factors among industries and the restructuring of resources in two countries due to the effects of a CK FTA. Here, some conclusions can be drawn. First, the demand changes for labor and capital in each sector, except a few, are expected to move simultaneously into the same direction, which means when labor demand increases, capital will follow. Second, the demand changes for both labor and capital in each sector are generously correspondent with their output changes in two scenarios, which means when sector output increases, the demands for the capital and labor will follow to increase, too. Third, in general, the demand changes for both labor and capita in each sector are expected to keep a basic synchronic movement between the two scenarios.

Compared to GTAP research conducted by KIEP (Hongshik Lee etc), this study shows a varying significance. First, the fundamental structures of CGE model are introduced in this paper, followed by a full and accurate explanation of GTAP analysis including production structures, demand structures and value linkages, as actually work as an essential prerequisite for the analysis framework. For reasons of streamlining my arguments, the GTAP production function was changed into Cobb-Douglas pattern in the final stage, together with aggregated primary factors for simplicity. Second, a more detailed model aggregation including the particularly defined region, sector classifications and factors used in this research is quite different from the KIEP study. Third, this study shows a more detailed analysis in sector levels. I investigate especially the effects of CK FTA on two countries' imports, exports, trade balance, outputs and demand changes for labor and capital on sectoral levels. Fourth, besides the relative changes by percentage of different endogenous variables such as welfare, GDP, trade and output revealed in this paper, their absolute volume changes due to CK FTA are also explored. Actually, even a large relative change reflects a very small variation if the initial volume, such as very small trade or output volume in some sector, changes in base data. The combination between the relative and absolute changes of endogenous variables would reveal a much clearer menu. Finally, the welfare gains in two scenarios are decomposed to explore the different sources of two countries' increased welfares, which help to fully understand the potential effects of a CK FTA.

Contents

CHAPTER
3   Economic Relations between China and Korea

CHAPTER
4 | Theoretical Analysis of the Korea-China FTA

| CHAPTER 6 | Conclusions |

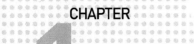

CHAPTER

1

Introduction

01 | Background of Free Trade Agreements (FTA)

Globalization has characterized the world economy in the recent years. The economic integration through freer trade and investment has progressed throughout the world. Regionalism is another major trend in economic integration. Most of the industrial and developing countries in the world have concluded some regional trade agreements. At present, more than one-third of world trade takes place under such agreements. In the Asia-Pacific region, regionalism took shape with the consolidation of the multi-national Asia-Pacific Economic Cooperation (APEC) accord at the end of the 1980s. The historic Bogor Declaration in 1994 set a target to achieve free trade and investment in the years 2010/2020. But in the 2000s, global circumstances have appeared to be changing. Economic integration is modifying its pattern in a broader and more profound background. The most significant change is that economic integration among different countries has broken regional framework, extending their counterparts to any country which is potentially beneficial for economic integration. Free trade agreements are developing very quickly, and are not just restricted to certain countries' regional partners.[1]

The concept of FTAs first appeared in 1947, the year when the General Agreement on Tariffs and Trade (GATT) was launched. The FTA is based on a provision in Chapter 24 of the GATT, which allows countries to push for free trade among themselves under certain conditions. GATT opened the way to freer international trade. It adhered to the basic principle of nondiscriminatory treatment among its contracting parties (Article 1, GATT), and its work to eliminate trade barriers was applicable to all member nations. However, in Article 24, it also approved of FTAs and other regional trade agreements as intermediate solutions toward freer globalized trade. Although such agreements, strictly speaking, violate GATT's nondiscriminatory principle, it was thought that such trade agreements would in the long run lead to global trade liberalization. On the basis of Article 24, the European Common Market was created which, more recently, has developed into the EU. Since then the NAFTA and many other FTAs have been concluded. GATT's efforts to promote global trade liberalization took the form of a series of multilateral trade negotiations, such as the Kennedy Round, the Tokyo Round, and the Uruguay Round. Although GATT evolved into the WTO in 1994, FTAs have continued to be formed in both developed and developing nations.

FTA requirements set forth by the GATT and WTO include the following five basic points. (a) When forming an FTA, member countries should not raise trade barriers against nonmember trading partners (*Article 24, Clauses 4 and 5 [b]*). (b) If an intermediate treaty is concluded, it should include plans and schedules to establish an FTA within a reasonable period (*Article 24, Clause 5 [c]*). According to the interpretation

---

1) Report and Policy Recommendations on Strengthening Trade Relations between China, Japan and Korea in joint-research of three research institutions.

The Feasibility of a Korea-China FTA and its Potential Economic Effects

of Article 24 agreed upon during the Uruguay Round, ten years has been determined as a "reasonable period." (c) Countries participating in an FTA should immediately notify GATT/WTO members of this fact (*Article 24, Clause* 7). (d) Within an FTA, customs tariffs and other restrictive trade rules and regulations should essentially be abolished for substantially all sectors (*Article 24, Clause 8 [b]*). (e) An FTA that includes trade in services should satisfy requirements similar to (a), (b), and (c) above which pertain to the commodity trade (*GATT Article 5, Clauses 1, 4, and 5–7*).[2]

The essential feature of a FTA is that it discriminates in favor of the interests of the agreement members. Under a FTA, barriers to trade, generally tariffs and quotas, are removed on trade between members, usually after a period of phase out. The result is that businesses in the member countries secure preferred access to the markets of other members over companies from non-members. Once FTAs go straight forward, they set out commitments to remove tariff and non-tariff barriers to trade in goods among the parties. Often they did not achieve 'free trade' but agreements to reduce barriers to agreed levels. Some are even, and more appropriately, called agreements on "Closer Economic Relations" rather than "Free Trade Agreements."[3] Today they cover much more than trade in goods. They cover services and investment and increasingly other areas to promote closer economic relations between countries.

---

2) GATT and WTO documents

3) A Report for the Department of Foreign Affairs and Trade by the Australian APEC Study Centre, Monash University August 2001.

02 | The Development of FTAs in the world

The world economy is far from "free" trade, although economists argue that free trade is the optimal trade policy in terms of welfare for the world population. Most countries, on one side, impose trade restrictions because of various reasons, including protection of their industries or political reasons. However, on the other side, countries seek to have unilateral, multilateral, and regional trade liberalization to increase their exports and also stimulate their economic growth.[4]

Many studies support that the countries which signed bilateral FTA will both benefit from economic interaction, which is good to increase production, good to domestic reform and improvement of the productivity, good to enlarge mutual investment and attract foreign investment, and good to the growth of GDP. Many scholars insisted on the view that bilateral FTA can push the multilateral trade liberalization forward to establish an open multilateral trading system. Bilateral FTA and multilateral trade system have the same objectives for trade liberalization to serve in different perspectives. From some points of view, bilateral FTA is one interim phase for chasing the trade liberalization. The economic globalization via trade liberalization is an inevitable historical trend.

In the more recent decades, the globalization process has entailed decisive policy changes. One of major global trends has been in the realms of trade interactions among countries. Along with the advent of the WTO, in contrast to previous decades, the last decade has witnessed

---

4) Hyun Joung Jin, Won W. Koo and Bongsik Sul, "The effects of the FTA among China, Japan and South Korea", *Journal of Economic Development*, Volume 31, Number 2, December 2006

a growth of regional trading arrangements (RTAs) at an unprecedented pace. There have been more than 250 free trade agreements (FTAs) around the world since 1948. Some of the FTAs include, for example, the European Union (EU), the Caribbean Community and Common Market (CARICOM), Southern Common Market (MERCOSUR), and the North American Free Trade Agreement (NAFTA). Recently the EU has strengthened its operation by adapting a common monetary system among its member countries and also expanding its membership from 15 to 27 countries. The United States also expanded its alliances by completing the US-Central America/Dominican Republic FTA and the US-Australia FTA, and initiating several other FTAs, including the free trade agreement with 33 Western Hemisphere countries, known as FTA of the Americas (FTAA), the US-Thailand FTA and US-Korea FTA and so on.

It is important to highlight that a major increase in the number of RTAs took place after 1995, and most of the RTAs happened in the form of FTAs. A rather well known fact is that around two-thirds of global trade is conducted on a preferential basis than the MFN (Most Favored Nation) principle. Therefore, any region can ignore formation of its own scheme of regional integration only at its peril as its exports would face discrimination against those of trade bloc members. Movement toward the establishment of FTAs at either the bilateral or regional level has recently intensified in the world. Economic integration through FTAs has become a global trend.

03 | Background of China-Korea Free Trade Agreement

In recent years, Northeast Asia has received growing attention as a region that has successfully begun with the process of integration into the global economy. While Korea is becoming a mature economy and catching up with Japan, China on the other hand, has emerged as an engine of growth, not only for Northeast Asia, but also for the whole world. The rapid trade between China and Korea has demonstrated broader prospects for regional cooperation. Despite all this, Northeast Asia is still characterized by its relatively lower level of regional integration, notwithstanding the fact that the economies in the region are to a large extent complementary and could potentially benefit from deeper economic integration. Until now, process toward forming a regional economic bloc such as FTA or PTA in Northeast Asia has been very slow since its inception. According to Yip,[5] Northeast Asia regionalism has been delayed owing to political factors rather than economic reason. Considering the increase in the trade interdependency among Northeast Asian countries, the need for an FTA in the region has gained high momentum in recent years. This has been reflected in a growing number of studies, which aim to explore the feasibility of an FTA in Northeast Asian countries, especially between Korea and China.

Both China and Korea have recently concluded or planned to pursue FTAs or negotiations with a sheer number of countries in the world.

---

5) Yip, W, "Prospects for Closer Economic Integration in East Asia," *Stanford Journal of East Asia Affairs1*, 2001, pp. 106-111.

For example, Korea has signed FTAs with Chile, Singapore, EFTA, and U.S, and has engaged in negotiations with many other countries such as Canada, EU and ASEAN countries. China has also concluded FTAs with Chile, ASEAN, Pakistan and New Zealand followed by many negotiating countries such as Australia, Central Asia Countries and so on. Based on research and discussions both China and Korea are now exploring the possibility to launch more FTA talks with other countries.

The Government-Industry-Academia Joint Study Meetings for a Korea-China FTA have been scheduled to take place many times. Partly due to the trend toward trade and investment liberalization in China, South Korea has faced a challenge with its massive production diversion to China. Such "industrial hollowing-out" or de-industrialization inside Korea may be proceeding, and may become a serious issue in terms of assuring domestic employment. The Korean economy needs to expedite economic reforms in order to help bring up new industries to absorb the displacement of the labor forces. Once an FTA which has been discussed is made between China and Korea, economic integration between the two countries will greatly change the trade and investment structures throughout Northeast Asia. Several existing studies have suggested that the most significant feature of the China-Korea FTA would be the promotion of an integration of firms, rather than a reduction of tariff rates. Therefore, due to FTA's influence, firm-level integration is expected to take place, which will lead to the creation and development of more excellent companies.

It would be mutually beneficial for the two countries to consider a common perspective to utilize the recent trend of liberalization. Proximity is an asset for the two countries to strengthen their relations through economic activities. The standard "gravity model" suggests that countries in near proximity with one another tend to trade and invest more. As far as trade is concerned, complementariness is highly with regard to bilateral trade between China and Korea. Moreover, the geographical location of the two countries may influence an optimal solution. As indicated above, Northeast Asian countries have not been involved in any regional trade arrangements, while the two mega-trade blocs, the EU and NAFTA have developed considerably. In light of the market size, population, technical accumulation, and many other economic aspects, huge potentials would exist in the integration of the two economies under investigation by this thesis.

Those bilateral and regional initiatives with possible FTA countries raise important questions concerning nation's interests and priorities in choosing a key FTA partner country. Based on the both China and Korea's economic and political relations in the East Asian Region, A China-Korea FTA should have been established much earlier than now. While China has express interest in launching Korea-China FTA negotiations, Korea has maintained that there needs to be a sufficient consideration of sensitive sectors, as the geographical proximity and similarity in production structures for agricultural and fishery products between Korea and China are likely to cause excessive damage to Korea's sensitive sectors. The upcoming Joint Study Meetings have been agreed upon based on the common understanding that such sensitive sectors should be exempted from liberalization under an FTA. The Korean side plans to emphasize its upholding of an FTA that is comprehensive, including not only trade in goods, services and investment, but also intellectual property rights, government procurement, and competition policy. Korea will also stress the need to provide full consideration for structurally weak and sensitive products such as agricultural and fishery items, especially rice. On the other hand, China is expected to want to limit the scope of the FTA to trade in goods, services, and investment, if possible, and instead emphasize strengthening industrial cooperation focused on technology transfer between the two countries.

04 | Paper Structures

The purpose of this study is to evaluate the feasibility of China-Korea FTA and its potential economic effects. In so doing, a computable general equilibrium model is employed for the analysis of FTA effects. The rest of the study is organized as follows. Chapter 2 analyzes the FTA strategies between Korea and China, and meanwhile compares their respective FTAs motivations in the similar and different perspectives. Chapter 3 offers a general background of the trade and economic relations between China and South Korea. Competitiveness and complementariness of Korea and China's Industries are compared and analyzed depending on relevant economic indices, which will seek common ground and understanding of trade and investment between China and Korea. Such a comparative analysis of bilateral trade and investment structure will help construct a future foundation to formulate a common perspective in FTA between the two economies. Chapter 4 covers an assessment of the feasibility of Korea-China FTA in its theoretical perspective. Chapter 5 details the GTAP model, its specification in this study, presents simulation results and analyzes the potential economic effects of the envisioned Korea-China FTA. Concluding comments are found in Chapter 6.

CHAPTER

2

A Comparison between Korea and China's FTA strategies

01 | Korea's FTA Strategy and Its Motivation

1.1. The Background of Korea's FTA strategy

With the rapid development of regional integration worldwide led by US and EU markets, the Korean government changed its traditional trade policy orientation which was based on multilateralism toward regionalism. Such a transition is mainly due to Korea's worrying about its being left out from the world-wide trends of preferential market opening. Since 2004 Korea has actively engaged in FTA negotiations. It has pursued comprehensive FTAs, covering all sectors and substantially all aspects of trade, in line with Article XXIV of GATT 1994, Article V of GATS and in certain areas beyond the WTO commitment. The main objective of pursuing FTAs is to secure better access to foreign markets, while at the same time creating growth momentum through accelerated trade liberalization in the domestic market.

The Korean government determined to pursue FTAs to complement the WTO's multilateral trading system after the Asian financial crisis.

Actually, official joint study groups for assessing FTAs between Korea and Japan begun to meet after Japanese Prime Minister Koizumi's March 2002 visit to Korea. In the ASEAN+3 Summit in Phnom Penh in November of 2002, Korea as well as China and Japan started seriously to discuss to establish FTAs. However, Korean FTA developing process lagged far behind other members of the WTO at a time when the FTA wave was spreading everywhere in the world. As a WTO member, Korea belongs to none FTA members before it concluded an accord with Chile in March 2004. In order to promote the FTA process, Korea formulated an FTA Roadmap in September 2003 and revised it in May 2004. Based on the Roadmap, Korea has been actively pursuing FTAs with over 20 countries.[6]

An important blueprint for Korea's FTA strategy triggered a series of initiatives. Since embarking on an ambitious FTA program in 2003, Korea currently has signed FTAs with Chile, Singapore, the European Free Trade Association (EFTA) and USA. The long-lasting Japan-Korea FTA negotiations have stopped since December 2004 due to many complicated hurdles. However, the U.S. and Korean governments have surprisingly been holding FTA negotiations since June 2006 and finally signed a Korea-USA FTA on April 2nd, 2007, with ratification from both governments still pending. This successful foray became a fresh start on Korea's FTA strategy, although it elicited a strong political reaction from anti-U.S. and anti-free trade protestors. In addition, Korea is also negotiating bilateral agreements with ASEAN, Canada, India, Mexico and MERCOSUR to check on the feasibility of FTAs in these regions.

For nearly a decade, South Korea has been transforming itself into

---

6) Korea's FTA Policy, Korean Ministry of Foreign Affairs and Trade, 2005.

an FTA hub in Northeast Asia. Signing a network of FTAs has been a key part of the national economic strategy of President Lee Myung-bak, a conservative, and his predecessor, the left-of-center Roh Moo-hyun. Both presented FTAs as necessary for advancing South Korea's economic well-being. Ongoing competitive pressure from Japanese firms, increased competition from Chinese enterprises, and the rapid ageing of the South Korean workforce have heightened the sense of urgency about boosting national competitiveness. President Lee has set a goal of building a "free trade network" that by 2014 would enable over 70% of South Korean exports to enjoy duty free access. He has explicitly tried to diversify the composition of South Korea's FTA partners, simultaneously negotiating FTAs with large advanced economies as well as with natural resource rich developing countries.

Korea and China have already conducted a joint study since 2005. And EU has also proposed a joint FTA research with Korea, starting in fall of 2006. Besides, Korea continued to pursue more FTAs with other possible countries like South Africa, MERCOSUR, Malaysia, Japan, and New Zealand and so on. They are all under consultation or study. Korea's vigorous multi-track FTA policy is not just to expand access to markets abroad for its export. On the other hand, establishing comprehensive and high-level FTAs with its main trading partners also represents Korea's sustained efforts to reform and open its domestic economy. Korea's FTA promotion is an integral part of its broader strategy of advancing to the next stage of economic development.

■ The Korea-Chile FTA

Chile was selected as Korea's first FTA partner in November 1998. After one year of preparation, negotiations started in December 1999. The Korea-Chile FTA was concluded in October 2002 and entered into force in April 2004. Since then, it has brought about a substantial increase (48.2 percent) in bilateral trade from 2004 to March 2005. Korea's exports of manufactured goods have increased to 47 percent, automobiles to 58 percent, and cellular phones to 250 percent.

■ The Korea-Singapore FTA

The Korea-Singapore FTA was substantially concluded in November 2004 and is expected to enter into force soon. It should be noted that the Korea-Singapore FTA included a provision recognizing goods produced in the Gaesong Industrial Complex in North Korea as originating in South Korea, which is crucial in securing export markets for goods produced in Gaesong.

■ Korea-EFTAN FTA

There were four rounds of negotiations before the Korea-EFTAN FTA concluded in July 2004, and it is predicted that it will be in force by the end of 2006. The Korea-EFTAN FTA is the first FTA with a developed regional bloc in Europe and thus will likely serve as a gateway for business people to access the European market for its next step.

■ Korea-EU FTA

After more than two years of negotiations, the European Union (EU) and South Korea signed a bilateral free trade agreement (FTA) on October 6, 2010. Both the South Korean National Assembly and the EU Parliament have ratified the agreement, and it is expected to go into effect provisionally on July 1, 2011. The South Korea-EU FTA (KOREU FTA) is the largest FTA in terms of market size that South Korea has entered into. The KOREU FTA reflects the EU and South Korean trade strategies to use FTAs to strengthen economic ties outside their home regions. It also builds upon the surge in trade and investment flows between South Korea and the EU over the past decade. The KOREU FTA is very comprehensive, generally mirroring the scope of the KORUS FTA, with some exceptions. The KOREU FTA would reduce and eliminate tariffs and other trade barriers in manufactured goods, agricultural products, and services and would also cover such trade-related activities as government procurement, intellectual property rights, labor rights, and environmental issues.

■ Korea-India FTA

The South Korea and India FTA was signed on August 7, 2009, dubbed the Comprehensive Economic Partnership Agreement (CEPA). The KIFTA came into force on January 1st, 2010. The negotiations took three-and-a-half years, with the first session in February 2006. The agreement will provide better access for the Indian service industry in South Korea including Information technology, engineering, finance, and the legal field. The CEPA will cut South Korean tariffs on 93% of goods from India. India will cut 75% of total tariffs South Korean car manufactures will see large tariffs cut to below 1%. The agreement will ease restrictions on foreign direct investments. Companies can own up to 65% of a company in the other country. Both countries avoided issues over agriculture, fisheries, and mining and choose not to decrease tariffs in those areas. This was due to the very sensitive nature of these sections in the respective countries.

■ Korea-US FTA

The United States and the South Korea signed the FTA on June 30, 2007. If approved, the Agreement would be the United States' most commercially significant FTA in more than 16 years. Under the FTA, nearly 95 percent of bilateral trade in consumer and industrial products would become duty free within three years of the date the FTA enters into force, and most remaining tariffs would be eliminated within 10 years. The FTA would immediately eliminate or phase out agricultural tariffs and quotas on a broad range of products, with almost two-thirds of Korea's agriculture imports from the United States becoming duty free upon entry into force. And the FTA would provide meaningful market access commitments for service that extend across virtually all major sectors, including greater and more secure access for international delivery services and the opening up of the Korean market for foreign legal consulting services. And the FTA would increase access to the Korean market and ensure greater transparency and fair treatment for U.S. suppliers of financial services. The FTA would address nontariff barriers in a wide range of sectors and includes strong provisions on competition policy, labor and environment, and transparency and regulatory due process.

■ Korea-Peru FTA

Korea has signed a FTA with Peru in Seoul on March, 21st, 2011 after two years of negotiations. And it will take effect on Aug. 1, 2011. Tariffs would immediately disappear for Korean televisions and certain automobiles. Peruvian coffee would benefit equally in Korea. And it will help Korea to bolster trade and investment and promote cooperation in resources development. From KPFTA, South Korea expected to expand into the South American markets

1.2. The Features of Korea's FTA Strategy

In response to the rapid proliferation of regionalism throughout the world, Korea has been actively pursuing FTAs with major trading partners. While remaining as a strong supporter of the multilateral trading system, Korea aims to pursue FTAs that are complementary to WTO liberalization. In this regard, Korea's FTA policy can be summarized as follows,

First, the Korean government announced its FTA policy direction as a 'simultaneous bilateral FTA formation', meaning that the negotiations can be carried out simultaneously with more than one country when necessary. Therefore, Korea's FTA strategy operates as a simultaneous multi-track basis with a comprehensive high-level.[7] The multi-track policy would help Korea jump on the free trade bandwagon which could ensure more benefits to its export-driven economy. From such a strategy, it can be inferred that Korea will continuously pursue several FTAs almost simultaneously rather than adopting a one-by-one approach. Korea believes this simultaneous approach can offset the negative effects caused by some FTA according to the positive impact caused by others. Korea intents to pursue a FTA Hub to benefit more from the trade diversion and trade creation process as FTA Hub-Spoke theory predicts.

---

7) Jeffrey J. Schott, Institute for International Economics, 2003.

Second, Korea propels FTA strategy with cautious steps before its pursuit of FTAs with large advanced economies, economic blocs and the promising emerging markets. Korea escalated its FTA counterparts step by step to form a long-term consistent FTA arrangement. At the initial stage of Korean government's efforts for FTA formation, the basic policy objection could be described as "maximization of the number of FTA agreements". Therefore, the preferred FTA partner countries for Korea have been the countries with the least political barriers or less potential economic effects in reaching the final agreement. As was demonstrated at the Cancun DDA meeting in 2003, the agricultural sector is one of the most actively organized interest groups against domestic market opening in Korea. Therefore, the Korean government started FTA negotiations with the partner countries that impose the least threat on agricultural market opening, such as Japan, Singapore, and Chile. Therefore, Korean FTA strategy could be considered as sequential or experimental. Although Korea made simultaneous FTAs with more than one country at the beginning, it selected its first FTA counterparts carefully. By initially fixing its future FTA partners, Korea carefully takes into account key factors such as economic benefits, political and diplomatic considerations, as well as domestic constraints including the vulnerability of the agricultural sector. These counterparts were investigated not only about their relatively smaller economic dimensions such as Chile, Singapore and EFTA but also about more details such as industry competition and possible adjustment costs during the process of FTA. Take Korea-Chile FTA as an example. The impetus that Korea chose Chile as its premier counterpart had many reasons including Chile's small economic scale, Chile's mature FTA experience and the opposite climate which may lessen the impact on the Korea's primary agricultural sectors from Chile's strong competition in these departments. After the initial stage, Korea began to pursue FTAs with giant economies and emerging markets such as U.S.A, EU, China and Mercosur.

Third, Korea aims to pursue FTAs that are high-level in terms of the degree of liberalization and comprehensive in terms of coverage and scope. In other words, Korea seeks to conclude FTAs that are consistent with the GATT/WTO rules. Article XXIV of the GATT sets the conditions under which FTAs can derogate to the Most Favored Nations (MFN) principle contained in Article I of the GATT. The main objective of Article XXIV was to prevent FTAs from becoming obstacles to the development of multilateral trade, but rather to make them a stepping-stone towards free trade. In order to do so, the provisions of the GATT regarding FTAs stipulated that they should not result in higher barriers to trade with third parties; they should also be ambitious in their scope and result in extensive trade liberalization. According to Article XXIV paragraph, FTAs should result in the elimination of duties and non-tariff barriers on "substantially all the trade". Korea's FTA Strategy was also comprehensive in its coverage, encompassing a wide range of areas such as services, investment, government procurement and intellectual property rights, in addition to trade in goods. Additionally, in order to achieve national consensus as part of the negotiation process, Korea aims to pursue a wide range of outreach efforts with the public and private sectors.[8]

---

8) Korea FTA Policy Division, MOFAT

1.3. The Motives of Korea's FTA strategy

A. Pursuing FTA as Defensive Approaches

By the mid-1990s, the world's leading economies except those in East Asia had become partners in FTAs. Indeed, both of the world's two largest economic regions − North America and Western Europe − all bonded in FTAs. As we all know, once a country has been excluded from FTAs, it will mostly suffer losses because of the trade diversion from the non-members to the bloc members. Once FTA goes into effect, the relevant market is effectively secured from competitors according to discriminative tariff rates which place non-member countries at a disadvantage. The possibility of being left out has promoted countries to engage in FTA talks with more countries as a protective measure. Suppose all prices are kept unchanged before and after FTA, while tariffs are eliminated on FTA members but maintained on all other countries, FTA countries will tend to buy more with one another and navigate away from goods consumption deriving from non-member countries. If goods are sufficiently strong substitutes, the goods demand for a third party will obviously decrease. Thus, in order to clear markets, the price of a third-party goods will have to fall, which will create a positive terms of trade effect for the member countries as long as no member country's price decreased by too much.[9] This course of action has been found by many results of CGE model's simulations and also by plenty of FTA practices.

FTAs concluded among other countries have resulted in discrimination

---

9) Mundell, R, "Tariff Preferences and the Terms of Trade," *Manchester School of Economic and Social Studies*, January, 1964, pp. 1-13.

against Korean enterprises. Disadvantages in market access are an example of this discrimination, just as Japan encountered in Mexico market. After the formation of NAFTA, Mexico's imports from Japan decreased by 50% annually, which made Japan, suffer a loss of 400 billion Yen each year. Therefore, Japan made a FTA with Mexico in March 2004 in order to offset such a loss due to the trade diversion. As the FTA between Mexico and Europe Came into effect, Mexico's customs tariffs on European automobiles had been reduced from 20% to zero until 2003. However, Korean automobiles in the Mexican market are losing price competitiveness because Mexican high import tariffs have continued to be applied to Korean products. In this regard, the conclusion of the Korea-Chile FTA will improve the price competitiveness of Korean products, enabling them to compete with other countries in the Chilean market better.

Thus, this potential "beggar thy neighbor" effect of FTAs can make an attractive proposition for potential members. Therefore, fear of isolation and losses is a major reason why countries pursue FTAs, and this trend has been expanding into a domino effect. The effect is common in Asia and Korea is no exception. Towards the tendency of FTA development, the Korea government began to realize that it was being discriminated against in many foreign markets. To overcome such a disadvantage and secure markets for its exports, Korea decided to implement its new FTA strategy without hesitation.

B. To Attracting Foreign Direct Investments (FDI) and Technology Transfer

The formation of region wide trading blocs by major trading nations of the world has implications for all other countries. The need to attract

FDIs is increasingly cited as an impetus for FTAs. Studies have showed that FTAs have emerged as major factors in determining the patterns of trade and investments. FTAs make their members more appealing destinations for domestic foreign investments and more competitive partners in trade at the disadvantage of non-members. Therefore, non-member countries have to respond by building their own FTAs to challenge the competitiveness coming from other blocs. Therefore, FTAs have become an important part of a country's strategic trade policy. The countries which are vigorously pursuing FTAs policy are also the ones which keep preaching to others the virtues of multilateralism to keep their edge gained by regionalism. Having built up their strong FTAs, the western countries are now trying to seek a moratorium on FTAs to protect their edge.[10]

Korea's stock of FDIs as a percentage of GDP is the lowest among OECD countries except for Japan. Just as Ethier states, "As a result of the East Asian financial crisis, Korea, already in the multilateral system, may well need to be able to attract direct investment in the future to remain there".[11] The empirical evidence linking FDI and economic growth is fairly robust. And numerous studies have confirmed and quantified the positive impact of FDIs on Korea. If Korea wants to position itself as a crucial Northeast Asia hub and benefit from the enormous opportunities in the region, it needs to put the highest priority on inviting FDIs. The establishment of FTAs could help to attract more FDI and lots of researches have testified FTA's positive effects on FDI. Korean government also expected to expand FDI depending on its

10) Balasubramanyam, V. N. and D. Greenaway, "Regional Integration Agreements and Foreign Direct Investment," Chapter 7 in K. Anderson and R. Blackhurst, 1993, pp.147-166.

11) Wilfred J. Ethier. "The Proliferation of Regional Trade Agreements and Its Rationale."

FTA-attracting success. FTAs could reduce distortions in production within its member countries and increase the size of the potential market. Furthermore, the FTAs could create a more stable and liberalized environment for the inflow of FDIs. The improvement of these investment factors could increase the overall quantity of foreign assets. As a matter of fact, NAFTA was created in 1994 mainly as an instrument to attract more and larger FDIs to the region at a time when competition for high volume asset flows was deemed to be increasing. Some have even described ASEAN-FTA as more of an investment pact than a trade pact.[12]

Countries have also been placing a strong emphasis on technology transfer in their multilateral and bilateral relationships, especially in developing countries. The development of this tend is universal, from the preponderance of requests for technical assistance in development aids and cooperation programs to the "virtuous cycle" of policy liberalization stemming from the desire to promote FDI inflows through reductions in transactions costs. In doing so, they expect to establish an attractive business environment within which multinationals can easily profit from a more efficient division of labor, as well as facilitating the emergence of multinationals within these countries. Of course, the same is true for Korea. According to the FTAs with developed countries, Korea will gain more from technology transfer, given the greater technological gap taking the form not only of production technologies, but also of management techniques, other business practices, corporate culture, and various training programs.

All in all, Korea has realized that FTAs are helpful in attracting FDI

---

12) Ariff, Mohamed, "Outlooks for ASEAN Externalities," in Shoji Nishijima, 1996.

CHAPTER 2. A Comparison between Korea and China's FTA strategies 41 and securing overseas footholds for the country's export. Korea must attract additional FDIs, not only for financial goals but for the acquirement of advanced technology and management skills from foreign companies. There is no doubt that the reduction of tariff and non-tariff barriers due to the FTAs will strengthen exporting capabilities among FTA members and improve Korea's production structure. By enabling Korean companies to adopt advanced technology from foreign companies, these innovations will then integrate rapidly with Korea's production and marketing capability. The development through FTAs with Korea's trading partners could even trigger new investments from ever more intrigued potential investment companies. In a sense, the Korean government is trying to utilize the FTAs as an important approach to attract FDIs and advanced technology.

C. Securing Export Market and Increasing Economies of Scale

Due to its relatively small domestic market size and scarce natural endowment, since the 1960s, Korea has mainly relied on overseas markets through an active export strategy to achieve its remarkable economic growth. Today, Korea's total external trade amounts to 70 percent of its GDP. FTAs could promote the country's sustained economic growth, which has been well proved theoretically and empirically. According to Christine McDaniel's research of the U.S. International Trade Commission, within four years implementing of KORUS FTA, Korean exports to the U.S. would increase by more than 20 percent.[13] The largest potential FTA gains for Korean exports to the United States have been anticipated in textiles, apparel, leather goods, and other manufacturing goods. Korean Trade Minister Kim Hyun-chong once believed FTAs are critical for the

---

13) Christine McDaniel, Alan Fox(2001)

country's economic growth and a more open economy with less trade barriers, which implies that a long-term FTA strategy will be necessary for the Korean economy to develop faster. The best solution at present is to have more FTAs that could give Korean companies greater access to foreign markets. Therefore, by joining a FTA and cooperating with other members, Korea can not only secure stable export markets and defend itself against discriminatory effects of other regional groups. In addition, if the potential FTA partner is a member of another type of FTA, it would be easier for Korea to gain access and diversify its exports to larger regional market.[14)]

On the other hand, the Korean products have gradually become less competitive facing the advanced technology of developed countries such as Japan, U.S.A and low-wage price competitiveness of developing countries such as China. Booz, Allen and Hamilton (1997) warned that Korea could be trapped in a "nutcracker" being caught between China's low costs and Japan's technical excellence. They stated that "Korea is too small to compete directly with either Japan or China over the long-term in its core industries."[15)] Moreover, liberalization is getting more difficult under the WTO framework. Given the situation, Korea became very interested in the FTA and its government viewed FTAs as a good opportunity to break the stalemate by making it as a policy option. FTAs can intensify the competition and force Korean industries to improve their competitiveness through technology development and the retrenchment of costs.

---

14) Jong-Heon Lee, Analysis: S.Korea's FTA push, 2005.

15) Booz, Allen and Hamilton, Revitalizing the Korean Economy towards the 21st Century. *Report for Vison Korea Committee.* Booz-Allen-Hamilton Inc. October, 1997.

A largely unmitigated beneficial effect that may be expected form FTAs stems from the increased size of the market leading to greater productive efficiency for any industry with economies of scale. As Krugman reminds us, the reason that turned the European Common Market into a strong economic success was the "huge intra-industry trade in manufactures, and the associated rationalization of production, that the Treaty of Rome made possible."[16] And since the Korean market is relatively smaller, access to larger markets is important in industries in which economies of scale are apparent. Modern technologies ensure that this is the case for many industries. FTAs can be used as a means to expand production at the margin and, hence, reap cost reduction benefits from the increased market size. The need to obtain economies of scale is often cited as an important goal to keeping economic growth robust.

D. Promoting Domestic Policy Reform and More Liberalization

Korean FTA strategy not only intends to provide gains in market access, but also to improve economic efficiency through competition. In many cases, FTA considerations were used as a strategy by policy makers to facilitate domestic reform and restructure.[17] FTAs presently have become a bridge to an open trade policy. WTO and many other international organizations have acknowledged FTAs as a contribution to the development of globalization. It has been widely accepted that FTA imply a stepping stone leading to the economic liberalization. The Korean government wants to use FTAs as an approach to realize its outward-oriented development strategy more openly and efficiently.

---

16) Krugman, Paul, "The Move Toward Tree Trade Zones," in Philip King, ed., *International Economics and International Economics Policy*: AReader (McGraw-Hill: New York), 1995, pp.163-186.

17) Zhang Yunling, "The Future Perspective of East Asian FTA," 2006.

Generally speaking, Korea's FTA policy dated from its financial crisis in late 1990's when the main economic purpose was to overcome the limited transparency of Chaebol economic operations. Korea had made good use of international frameworks such as IMF to bring it through the financial crisis. External pressure, especially from the United States has helped to reform Korean industries, institutions, and policies. Indeed, structural reform contributed significantly in recovering Korea's economy and helped improving the competitiveness of its manufacturing sector. In the process of overcoming the financial crisis, the government keenly realized that reform and liberalization policies are crucial to raise international credit ratings and that such policies had to be continued after the crisis in order to maintain Korea's significant role in the global economy. However, after the crisis transition, Korean economy increased slowly while its domestic economic reform appeared tardy due to many impediments from outdated economic structures. And Korean economic reforms have encountered many difficulties in many aspects, including a radical reduction in regulations; the corporate reform to loosen the grip of the Chaebol; the reform in the country's highly inefficient labor market and the reform of liberalization in its domestic market. These difficulties could be very difficult to solve under the old systematic framework.

In order to solve these problems, the best way will rely on speedier economic development toward a freer international market. With this in mind, FTAs were seen as the best approach to reach Korean reform goals through the characteristic of openness and liberalization. The benefits of an FTA not only extend credibility in the area of trade reform but also spill over into micro and macroeconomic reforms domestically. FTAs can generate gains as a means of promoting deregulation and structural reform, competition policy and government procurement, which could enforce a stronger market orientation and inspire greater microeconomic competition by reducing the power of domestic monopolies and their "rent seeking" efforts. Meanwhile lawmakers should put constraints on government spending by abolishing export subsidies and restrictions on industrial policies, as noted in DeMelo and Panagariya(1992).[18]

With the strongly increasing competition from MNCs, the likely strategy for Korea's enterprises to compete internationally is to orientate toward a global scoop and confront all challenges. FTAs also supply less competitive industries with a buffer zone before they suffer a great calamity with a full global liberalization. In this sense, FTAs actually work as an accidental insurance which could import moderate competition from foreign countries to push and force the domestic industries to accelerate reform and structure adjustments.

E. Increasing Macroeconomic Stability

There is general consensus in economics that macroeconomic stability is critical to the continued success of any development strategy. Even short-term bouts of instability can haunt an economy for many years to overcome. The financial crisis in 1997 was accompanied by serious economic sufferings among Korean people. But it has provided a series of good lessons for the government to think more deeply about the financial stability problems. Taking in these lessons, Korea's government has realized it's quite difficult to maintain and promote independent macroeconomic stability. Making use of external means to support this

---

18) De Melo, Jaime, and Arvind Panagariya, "New regionalism," *Finance and Development*, 29, December, 1992.

trend is probably a necessary part of the stabilization process. In this sense, the most important contribution that FTAs can make to Korea is to help support stable macroeconomic policies. Moreover, FTAs provide more options to help encourage macroeconomic stability. In order to ensure a stable partnership, member countries must share information, cooperate in advocating stable fiscal and monetary policies, and engage in strong "peer pressure" against unstable policies. Therefore, financial framework and links under FTA would lead to stable macroeconomic policies if the agreement is to function smoothly.

F. Strengthening the Political or Strategic Alliances

All existing formal FTAs were either created as economic arrangements in support of political goals or in consistency with diplomatic strategy of the founding countries. Usually, Economic cooperation could be seen in FTAs as an important vehicle to reach more pronounced bilateral or multilateral political goals. More FTAs could provide a more stable economic environment withstanding possible global political shocks for its members. Furthermore, FTAs are expected to spill into diplomatic cooperation, covering a wide range of important issues such as security, environment, labor and cultural exchanges. In such diplomatic spirit, the Korean government adopted its trade policy goal toward becoming the business hub and commercial gateway of Northeast Asia and the Pacific Rim.

Korea has many existing qualities that would make it a suitable centre for such a regional hub, including its ideal geographic location, world-class infrastructures, and human capital with high-quality. However, Korea is currently far behind reaching its goal but is using FTA strategy and ongoing reforms to catch up with it. Furthermore, FTAs may give Korea a stronger hand in its future trade negotiations with the greater regional powers. Therefore, Korea's FTA strategy could help to increase its influence on international affairs, strengthen its bargaining position and enhance its diplomatic weight.

02 | China's FTA Strategy and Its Motivation

2.1. The Background of China's FTA Strategy

Since the 1990s, FTAs have become popular trade policies of governments and hot topics for academic research. Following the worldwide trend, China has gradually adopted bilateralism, and pursued formal negotiations and informal studies toward creating FTAs with their trading partners. China's excursion into FTAs can date back to the end of last century and really expanded irreversibly soon after its access to WTO. Compared to the FTA strategies of both Japan and America, "China's FTA strategy is not as explicit as enough. China has not shown its clear stance on what kind of FTA goals should be implemented in East Asian and also has no specific evaluation and conceptions about the economic impacts after the opening of China's market. China's researching and preparation towards FTA has not been sufficient and eloquent until now."[19] However, during recent years, especially starting in 1999, China has accelerated its developing pace for FTAs and a gradually delineated a clearer FTA-policy approach which can be seen from government's series of actions.

---

19) 赵晋平，"FTA我国参与区域经济合作的新途径2，中国国务院研究中心，调查研究报告，第76号，总1925号，2003年7月.

Although the multilateral trading system remains the main channel to promote trade liberalization, China has been intensifying its pursuit of bilateral/regional free trade agreements with different trading partners over the last decade. For China, regional and bilateral trade arrangements serve as another driving force to promote free trade. Currently, China is working on 14 FTAs with 35 economies, among which 9 free trade agreements have been signed. Another 5 agreements including the China--GCC13 FTA, the China-Australia FTA, the China-Iceland FTA, the China-Norway FTA and the China-SACU FTA are being negotiated or are under discussion. The joint feasibility studies of the China- India RTA and the China-Korea FTA have been completed. The studies of China--Switzerland FTA and China-Japan-Korea FTA are underway. The concluded and signed FTAs or trade agreements with FTA features are the Mainland and Hong Kong Closer Economic and Partnership Arrangement (CEPA Mainland-Hong Kong), the Mainland and Macao Closer Economic and Partnership Arrangement (CEPA Mainland-Macao), the China-ASEAN FTA (ACFTA), the China-Pakistan FTA, the China- Chile FTA, the China-New Zealand FTA, the China-Singapore FTA, the China-Peru FTA and the China-Costa Rica FTA. Currently, China is involved with 'simultaneous multi-track' negotiations with many countries in the world. And its FTA map has gradually moved forward and pragmatically proceeded in different ways with different partners. Also, these negotiations represent progressive engagement and development of inter country relationships as much as precise text with clearly defined and precisely articulated commitments. Agreements go well beyond trade and services, and cover many areas of cooperation not even involved in WTO recommendations.

On the other hand, China is carrying out an authentically native

FTA Strategy that can be described as "Advance Gradually and Secure Easy Things First while Leaving Difficult Things for Later". As for this "the gradual advance" strategy, China tends to carefully weigh advantages and disadvantages, and then gradually opens the signature page toward an FTA conclusion. In this way, china accumulated its first trade negotiation experiences with the "earlier" Asian countries first in terms of its "FTA-making path". The rule of "the easy first, difficult later" can be well comprehended from its FTA strategy among China, Japan and South Korea. Among the three countries, It is reasonable to expect the bilateral FTA between China and Japan to be full of difficulties. One is the most developed country in Asia, the other is the biggest developing country. Theoretically speaking, the signature of an FTA between China and Japan would lead to significant mutual benefits, but there are many complications waiting to be solved. The unaddressed issue of Japanese war atrocities committed against China during World War II leaves a keen sense of distrust before "free trade" ought to become beneficial for Japan. Therefore, the prospect of an FTAs signature between China and Japan still is vague while a CK FTA could be expected in the short run for its relatively less blocks.

■ The CEPA Mainland-Hong Kong and the CEPA Mainland-Macao

In 2003, the Central Government of China signed the Closer Economic Partnership Arrangements (CEPA) with the Government of the Special Administrative Region of Hong Kong and the Government of the Special Administrative Region of Macao respectively. The CEPA Mainland-Hong Kong, the CEPA Mainland-Macao and the Supplements thereto cover trade in goods, trade in services and investment. The CEPAs were the first FTAs implemented in Mainland China. According to the CEPAs and their Supplements, Mainland China eliminated gradually the tariffs on imports originated from these two Special Administrative Regions (SARs) from 1st January 2004 on, completed by 1st January 2006. Under these CEPAs, Mainland China has also gradually liberalized markets in various service sectors by relaxing market access restrictions.

■ The China-ASEAN FTA

On 4th November 2002, China and ASEAN signed the Framework Agreement on Comprehensive Economic Cooperation, which entered into force on fist July 2003. Under the Frame- work Agreement, both Parties agreed to negotiate a China—ASEAN Free Trade Area (ACFTA) which was supposed to be fully established within ten years. Both Parties also promised to progressively eliminate tariffs and non-tariff barriers to the great majority of merchandises, simplify customs procedures, progressively liberalize trade in services, and establish open and competitive investment regimes to facilitate and promote investments. The Agreement on Trade in Goods and the Agreement on the Dispute Settlement Mechanism of the Framework Agreement on Comprehensive Economic Cooperation between ASEAN and China were signed in November 2004 and entered into force on 1st January 2005. According to the Agreement on Trade in Goods, China has been gradually reducing tariffs on thousands of goods to zero originated from ASEAN members. The Agreement on Trade in Services of the China-ASEAN Free Trade Area was signed in January 2007 and entered into force on 1st July 2007, under which China will lower the market access requirements of some service sectors including construction, environmental, transportation, sporting and business services, etc. In August 2009, the two Parties signed the Agreement on Investment which will facilitate the two-way investment and strengthen the relevant cooperation.

■ The China-Pakistan FTA

In April 2005, China and Pakistan announced the launch of FTA negotiations. The China- Pakistan FTA was signed on 24th November 2006 and entered into force on 1st July 2007. After its enforcement, China's overall average tariff on imports from Pakistan was 2 percentage points lower than the overall MFN average. On 21st February 2009, China signed the Agreement on Trade in Service of the China-Pakistan FTA which entered into force on 10th October 2009. According to the Service Agreement, China shall reduce restrictions on 6 service sectors including environmental services, tourism services, sporting services, translation services, real estate services, computer services, etc.

■ The China-Chile FTA

On 18th November 2005, China and Chile signed the China-Chile Free Trade Agreement which entered into force on 1st October 2006. Under the FTA, 63% of China's import tariffs were eliminated by two phases between 1st October 2006 and 1st January 2007. Most other tariffs are to be eliminated within five or ten years with the aim of 97% of Chinas' import tariffs being eliminated by 1st January 2015. Negotiations on trade in services and investment were launched in January 2007. The Supplementary Agreement on Trade in Services of the Free Trade Agreement between China and Chile was concluded on 13th April 2008. China will re-lease market access restrictions in 37 service sectors including computer services, advertisement services, air transport services, sporting services, etc.

■ The China-New Zealand FTA

On 7th April 2008, China signed the China-New Zealand Free Trade Agreement which entered into force on 1st October 2008. The Agreement covers areas of trade in goods, trade in services and investment. The Agreement is the first FTA China signed with a developed country. Under the FTA, China will eliminate tariffs on 96% of imports originated from New Zealand. On 1st October 2008, when the FTA took effect, China immediately eliminated the tariffs on all the goods of which MFA tariffs were below 5%. The tariffs on other goods have been gradually reduced since 2008. China will also offer more favorable market access condition to New Zealand service suppliers in sectors of business services, environmental services, sporting services, transportation services, etc.

■ The China-Singapore FTA

The China-Singapore Free Trade Agreement (CSFTA) was signed on 23rd October 2008 and entered into force on 1st January 2009. The CSFTA covers trade in goods and in services. According to the CSFTA, China committed to eliminate the tariffs on 97.1% of goods imported from Singapore from 1st January 2010 and to further open up the market of the ser- vice sectors including health services, education services, accounting services, etc. on the basis of its WTO commitment.

■ The China-Peru FTA

The China-Peru FTA was signed on 28th April 2009 and came into force on 15th January 2010. Under the agreement, China shall eliminate the tariff on 90% of goods originated from Peru which include aquatic products, minerals, fruits, etc. China also took the commitment to further open up its service sectors of the mining services, consultation services, translation ser- vices, sporting services, tourism services, etc.

■ The China-Costa Rica FTA

Costa Rica is China's second largest trading partner in Central America while China is the second largest trading partner of Costa Rica globally. In recent years, bilateral trade between the two countries has grown steadily. In June 2007, China and Costa Rica established diplomatic relations. In November 2008, the Chinese President HU Jintao visited Costa Rica and announced together with the Costa Rican President Oscar Arias the launch of China- Costa Rica free trade negotiations. The China-Costa Rica FTA was signed on 8th April 2010.[20]

2.2. The Motives of China's FTA Strategy

The many commonalities that would underline a free trade relationship between Korea and China will be outlined in the following section where the characteristics of China's FTA strategy will be elaborately analyzed.

A. Defensive Consideration

China's view on FTAs has changed from earlier skepticism to active participation. Up until recently China maintained a steadfast support for trade liberalization realized only through multilateral means, such

---

20) China FTA Network

as through WTO and APEC venues. However, as countries of almost all regions have embraced regionalism, China has to question its previous FTA stance which would make it lose out to the substantial trade diversion of these growing agreements. Especially after the Asian monetary crisis, the problems of economic stability and the proliferation of RTAs as well as preferential trade agreements (PTA) have become an urgent topic for the Chinese government to confront. Following the setback of WTO negotiations in December 1999, China began to shift its previous FTA policy and actively favored the development of FTAs by quickly broadening its FTA partner range. The Chinese scholars Long and Zhang (2002) explain China's FTA policy by describing two aspects: unilateral trade liberalization and promotion of an institutional regional economic cooperation system after realizing the drawback during the East Asian Economic Crisis. China expects to sign FTAs with its main trading partners as a way to cope with the negative effects from other economic blocs and to response to the trend of proliferating FTAs in the world economic arena.[21]

China has been developing a sense of profound cooperation both in bilateral and multilateral FTA development and tries to get rid of the nearsighted behavior basing on over-political demands. In order to stimulate bilateral and multilateral FTAs and to attract more countries to join, China is carefully improving its relevant trade institutions.

B. Economic Consideration

China's recent keen interest in FTAs appears to have a long-term

---

21) Long, Guoqiang and liping Zhang, "China: From Open Regionalism to Institutional Regional Arrangement?". Presented at the KIEP's International Conference on Prospects for an East Asia FTA, Seoul, September, 2002.

strategic consideration both from an economic and a political perspective. It is obvious that China now sees FTAs as a crucial means to enhance its economic development through expanding China's market size. China is also establishing market coordination mechanisms to improve the investment environment so as to attract more investments from outside the region. This is in line with Beijing's need to guarantee the supply of energy and raw material from ASEAN to help diversifying export markets.[22]

From bilateral FTAs, China expects to be offered more preferential treatment than it currently receives from the WTO. Lower tariffs and non-tariff barriers from the preferences would help to lower the cost of trade and improve China's market access in order for Chinese firms to obtain cheaper raw materials and equipments. Under preferential trading conditions, Chinese Customers could also gain better access to cheaper and higher quality goods and services. Furthermore, FTAs lead to the expansion of trading markets, the formation of more efficient industrial structures and the improvement of competitive environments.

Since the mid-1980s, intra-regional East Asian trade (excluding Japan) has been growing at twice the rate of growth than that of world trade. Intra-regional trade patterns have shifted dramatically from trade in primary products to intra-industry trade in manufactures, especially IT products. There are fast-growing regional production-sharing arrangements involving trade in parts and components, especially electrical and electronic parts, office machinery and telecommunications equipment. After Japan, China has been the largest regional importer of parts and components, which are actively promoted through tariff exemptions.[23]

22) Ravenhill and Jiang, 2007, p19.

Another key point of China's FTA strategy is to get wider acceptance of 'market-economy-status'. After 20 years' reform and opening up, the market economy system in China has greatly improved, and the production and operation modes of its enterprises has gradually become consistent with the general requirements of a market economy. At present, China is pushing hard for removal of its non-market economy status. Actually, many countries, such as Singapore, Malaysia, Thailand, New Zealand and Australia have already accorded China full market-economy status. The other ASEAN countries did the same recently in a joint statement.[24] However, as the most important trade partners, neither America nor EU has acknowledged China's market economy status until now. It is not accidental that China is in or talking about FTA negotiations with the countries that have conceded market-economy status. This is bound to be a central Chinese demand if FTA talks begin with countries outside the region.

With a rapid economy increase, the Chinese government is now highly concerned about national security in terms of energy. As a result, China's FTA policies sometimes seek to satisfy too many of the country's own specific needs. A planning FTA with GCC can be a good explanation for China's energy consideration. An FTA with GCC will greatly help to solve China's energy problem.

C. Political and Strategic Consideration

The reason that China is deeply absorbed in bilateral trade negotiation

---

23) Francis Ng and Alexander Yeats, 2003.

24) "China full market economy: ASEAN", 2004.

considerations is partly because of political rationales. China aims to strengthen the political relations among countries through regional cooperation or economic connections. Through signing bilateral FTAs, China could strengthen its diplomatic relations and find more allies to reach its political objectives. Therefore, China considers FTAs as a useful strategy which could help reduce the potential political frictions. This strategy would help expand and harmonize existing international regulations and systems in East Asia. Nowadays, China appears to be smoothing its relations with the United States while pursuing its own political dominance in East Asia. China tried to create FTAs as a good approach to secure political and economic influences within the larger context of the construction of a regional system. In this perspective, priority should be given to conclude FTAs within Asian countries which, besides close economic relationships, have relatively important political relations and influences to protect. East Asia could well become the region with the most promising counterparts for negotiations. Accordingly, we can conclude that except for ASEAN, the Republic of Korea is the most likely FTA partner for China's FTA plans for the next future negotiations.

On the other hand, FTAs will increase China's bargaining power in WTO negotiations. The deepening of economic interdependence gives rise to political trust among countries that are parties to these agreements, which could suit China's global diplomatic influence and interest well. Meanwhile, China's new FTA strategy can also be considered as a means to defeat the Taiwan's separation. The leaders of Taiwan have always made its economic contact especially FTA with other countries as its policy to further withdraw from China. Therefore, a comprehensive Chinese FTA strategy can effectively prevent Taiwan's continued separation and contribute to peace and prosperity in the region.

03 | A Comparison of Korea and China's FTA Strategies

3.1. Both FTA Strategies Share Multi-track Basis but Have Different Features

Above all, both Korea and China's FTA strategies share simultaneous multi-track, but have different features with the selection of their FTA counterparts. Both China and Korea pursued their several FTAs with more than one country almost at the same time rather than adopting a one-by-one approach. Both countries believed this simultaneous approach can benefit more offsetting the negative effects caused by FTAs. However, Korea and China's emphases on their FTA partners are oriented differently. China's FTA strategy is directed at its East Asian neighborhood, covering both northeast and Southeast Asia. Its motives are both geopolitical and economic, which means China's neighboring countries remain a focal point as its FTA counterparts. As we all know, China always considers its neighbors as its most important strategic and political partners. Such an FTA policy is absolutely consistent with China's diplomatic policies, which always orient its neighboring countries as the starting point of international strategy. Although China is preparing to expand its FTA counterparts outside Asia at present, focusing on Australia-China and New Zealand-China FTAs and so on, but China's neighboring countries will continuously be locked in as core partners of its FTA plans.

But on the Korean side, the situation is quite different. Korea requires the exterior forces to balance its relations with regional big powers such as China and Japan in view of its relatively smaller economic and political power in East Asia. Correspondingly, Korea's FTA policies don't confine only within Asia but spread to Europe, North America, Latin America, even Oceania, in order to pursue its economic and strategic purposes. Korea now has several ratified FTAs with Chile, Singapore and EFTA, most of which are non-Asia countries. Therefore, Korea's FTA strategy which mainly focused its goals on the economic perspective can't be easily prejudged as a reflection of regionalism while it has more profound meanings varying from liberalism to realism.

3.2. Both FTA Strategies are affected by Liberalization Process

Both Korea and China's FTA strategies share the same difficulty of unilateral liberalization and the slow progress in multilateral trade liberalization under the WTO. This background served as a strong external impetus having triggered both countries' FTA strategies. Unilateral liberalization of a country's economy, especially for Korea, is unlikely to be a time consistent policy. Unilateralism is thus less effective due to the distinct liberalization degrees among their industries. The temptations to provide protection to its frail economic sectors, mainly in Korea' primary sectors are likely to be large, either because of income distributional reasons for political economy concerns, or for terms-of-trade considerations. Although China has an advantage of a low-wage labor force, unilateral liberalization has proved to be a challenging process. Without any concession from its competitors or some special motives with some urgent demand just as what Mexico did before it entered the NAFTA, it's hard to imagine a smooth process of unilateral liberalization.

An FTA, by paying the possible cost even for a small deviation from agreed trade liberalization, makes the small temptations that culminate in an overall distorted economy easier to overcome. Thus, a country in an FTA will face the cost of either exiting from the agreement, or an agreed upon large punishment from the other members, should it extend protection to some particular sector of its economy.[25] Accordingly, the shortcomings exist under the unilateral liberalization framework can be well overcome convincingly under the FTA process.

As to WTO multilateral negotiation process, With 149 nations in 2007, each with a veto over any final deal, negotiating new or improved rules of trade is inevitably a complicated and difficult business. Despite years of multilateral efforts, trade liberalization under the WTO has become increasingly difficult and a slow process. With the increase in the number of WTO members, there has been a growing divergence of views on the pace and the extent of trade liberalization. The increasing difficulty in reaching consensus on trade issues, for example, delayed the start of a new sequence of talks after the Uruguay Round. A more devastating example exists since July 23, 2006 when the completion of the Doha Round had to be declared impossible in the short run. On that day, the negotiations stalled on agriculture owing to the gap that appeared among the countries of the G-6, namely Australia, Brazil, India, Japan, the EU. The American trade Director-General, Pascal Lamy, said he did not know how long the talks will be suspended. They can only resume when progress

---

25) Raquel Fernandez, "Returns to Regionalism: An Evaluation of Non-Traditional Gains from RTAS", NBER Working paper series, National Bureau of Economic Research 1050 Massachusetts Avenue Cambridge, MA 02138 March 1997.

has been made, which in turn will require changes in entrenched positions. The suspension will apply to all negotiating groups. In a speech before the International Trade Committee of the European Parliament in Brussels on 17 October 2006, Lamy said "the failure of the trade talks would not be a major economic shock that precipitates any particular market crisis ... but rather as a slowly developing disease that would progressively sap the strength of the multilateral trading system built up over the past 50 years, damaging its economic lungs, its political heart, and its systemic bone structure."[26]

There is no necessity to declare multilateralism dead, just because this round of Doha talks is over, but the frustration over the Doha negotiation really promotes the FTA's development and proliferation. Faced with the failure of Doha negotiation and the current impossibility of managing trade liberalization on a global scale, many countries get fed up with free trade altogether and opted to forming FTAs with like-minded countries to open their trade regimes and so did the Korea and China.[27]

China and Korea's domestic political powers react differently towards the FTA process. In China, due to its highly centralized decision regime and the obscure voices from its interest groups, the struggling among the different interest groups is not evident. Many reactions to its FTA strategy are just constrained to behaviors of the government. While the Korean political situation is quite different, Korea's interests groups are well established and organized. Its various labor unions, especially some agricultural federations, have a strong influence on government decisions.

---

26) http://www.wto.org/english/news_e/news06_e/mod06_summary_24july_e.htm
27) Http://news.bbc.co.uk/1/hi/business/5215318.stm

Thus, the FTA process in Korea is not only an international negotiation procedure, but a struggling one, involving many obligations to make concessions, on domestic political levels.

3.3. Both FTA Strategies have Profound Political Considerations

Both countries' FTA strategies contain careful political considerations but in different ways serve their specific purposes. As we have analyzed above, the Korean government fashioned its trade policy in terms of becoming the business hub of Northeast Asia. But China also intends to use FTAs to reinforce its weight and establish leadership credentials in East Asia. China strongly emphasized its interests with ASEAN on a comprehensive level. This is Why China takes ASEAN as an integrated region to make a China-ASEAN FTA. A stable and cooperative ASEAN will well serve China's interest in creating a peaceful peripheral environment, which is crucial for its transition toward the modernization.28) As a result of development and advancement of China-ASEAN FTA, ASEAN countries' worries and misgivings about China have been replaced with trust, admiration, and respect.29)

One of reasons for China to actively pursue FTAs is a response to the challenges from Japan's FTA strategy. Japan has formulated a clear FTA strategy since 2002 and has been dealing in FTAs with ASEAN and other countries in East Asia. According to FTA theory, once a FTA

---

28) Yoriko Kawaguchi's policy speech, " Building bridges toward our future: Initiating for reinforcing ASEAN integration,", June 17,2003.

29) Ying Chengde, "东盟外交新走向：兼论中国与东盟关系", [东盟外交新趋势：中国与东盟关系], 国际问题研究, International Studies] Vol. 3 (2004), p.24.

has formed, it would generously cause the negative trade diversion on non-members. If China were excluded from a large scale FTA in East Asia, which was led by Japan, China's trade would be squeezed considerably. Finally its economy will become deteriorated just owing to the trade diversion effects. "It has been widely recognized that both China and Japan have been rivals for the leadership of the East-Asia region. In this sense, one would suspect that China is actively pursuing the FTA with Korea and other countries in an attempt to hold back the rapid expansion of FTAs between Japan and other countries in this region. This is reflected by the fact that China is actively promoting economic cooperation with ASEAN while agreeing on an Early Harvest Program with relatively unfavorable terms for China's agricultural sector."[30]

As for Korea, although Korea has not maintained a good political relationship with Japan due to historical or territorial problems, it still pursued an FTA with Japan. In 2007, Korea has signed an Korea-US FTA, which also exhibits Korean strong political consideration on its FTA strategy. With KORUS FTA, Korea partially intends to strengthen the military alliance between the two countries.

3.4. Korea's FTA Process has a Comparative Advantage on its Strategic Tactics

From the perspective of FTA implementations, Korea's FTA strategy is both cautious and deliberate, which can be observed from two aspects, namely the sufficient preparations before an FTA and the choices of its initial FTA counterparts. In order to promote the FTA, Korea formulated

---

30) Hongshik Lee, Hyejoon Lm, Inkoo Lee, Backhoon Song, Soonchan Park. By KIEP (Korean Institute for International Economic Policy), December, 30, 2005.

its FTA Roadmap in September 2003 and revised it in May 2004. Korea enacted the "Presidential Directive on Procedures for the Conclusion of FTAs" to smoothen the process and generate public endorsement in June 2004.

Regarding the selection of partner countries, the most important factor Korea has to think about is to create an FTA network with large markets. Korea's ultimate goals are the maximization of economic benefits and the advancement of its economic structure. However, networking with leading economies would bring huge spillover effects and confront huge risks. For the sake of safety, Korea selects its counterparts depending on the partner's relative advantages and economic features. Furthermore, Korea has always sets its timetables for long-term studies and negotiation periods until all evident disputes could be solved. If confront some harsh problems, Korea would rather suspend them and thus never advance in large joint-ventures. The Korea-Japan FTA is a good example for this.

The Korea-Chile FTA proved the advantageous effects in all areas mentioned above. During the eleven months after the deal's ratification by the end of March 2006, the volume of exports to Chile more than double. In contrast, neither the rise of Chilean agricultural imports to Korea nor the negative impacts resulting from it were seen as greatly significant. As a whole, the country is experiencing concrete gains as a result of the FTA. A close look at bilateral trade over the past eleven months shows that the concerns about the expected effects on the agricultural sector have been unnecessary. At the time of the conclusion of the Korea-Chile FTA, the Korean agricultural sector was expected to suffer a loss of 586 billion won over ten years, at an average of 58.6 billion won per year. However, during the eleven months after the conclusion of the FTA, increases in agricultural imports were 5.78 billion won, only 10% of the amount expected. Moreover, 92.5% (5.34 billion won) of this was due to the increase in the import of wine. Therefore, excluding the increase in wine imports, the actual loss only amounts to 440 million won.

As to China, until now, there is still no officially announced FTA strategy and there is no specialized authority in charge of FTA preparations. Most of the FTA business is managed by Ministry of Commerce of PRC which lacks in the ability to coordinating and harmonizing sources of different departments. Compared to Korea, China owns insufficient intellectual sources for FTA research. Scientific and overall empirical studies have not been prepared well before practical negotiation steps were taken. Therefore, it is hard to learn about the possible effects of FTAs on different industries and take relevant measures in advance. The China-ASEAN FTA is a case to prove this. For example, China agreed to an EHP (Early Harvest Program) with ASEAN on relatively unfavorable terms for the Chinese agriculture sectors of vegetables and fruits. Due to the EHP effect, vegetables and fruits imported from Thailand had sharply increased by 38% and 80% respectively during the first six months in 2004, which caused a severe attack on Chinese farmers producing such food commodities.

04 | Summary

Both Korea and China's FTA strategy share a similar international background. For the time being, FTA has become a popular and relatively level field on which countries can align economic cooperation. China and Korea have adapted FTA as their significant economic strategies to develop and improve their economies. Looking at the two countries' economic backgrounds will help us to comprehend their FTA strategies. Above all, both countries' FTA strategies have defensive motives. An FTA can reduce tariffs and non-tariff barriers and stimulates trade for member nations. In an effort to avoid the negative effects of being excluded from such agreements, and to actively cope with proliferating regionalism, both Korea and China have decided to pursue FTAs with other nations.

Besides, two countries' FTA strategies were driven both by exterior stimuli such as the stagnation of WTO process along with FTA proliferation and by interior factors like trade expansion, FDI attraction, its industry reform structures, the promotion of benign competition and the efficient allocation of the resource. The two countries' FTA strategies thus reflect carefully rationalized long-term economic, political, and strategic goals. In theoretical terms, these goals are tested and verified from the perspectives of trade diversion, trade creation, domino theory, and hub-and-spoke theory.

Furthermore, both countries' FTA strategies are consistent with WTO rules. Just as with Korea's FTA strategy, until now China's FTA initiatives have always run by rules and framework of WTO. Namely, the two countries' FTA strategies didn't come at the expense of its very strong commitment to WTO. Rather they are seen as complementary. Both countries never gave up the struggle for the integration and advancement of multilateral free trade under the WTO framework or other international cooperation rules.

CHAPTER

3

Economic Relations between China and Korea

01 | Trade and Investment Patterns between Korea and China

1.1. Trade Status Quo between Korea and China

In this chapter, I examine the changes that have taken place in the export structure of China and Korea and their implications for their bilateral trade relationship. Because of the cold war and other political reasons, for a long time, there was no direct trade beside small-scale trade transiting through Hong Kong, Singapore and other regions. It was not until 1988 when non-governmental direct trade began to increase gradually. On August 24, 1992, diplomatic relations were tied between China and Korea, which established a basis for the increase and development of bilateral trade between them. This new relationship led to a series of agreements in economic, trade and technological cooperation. Thus the two countries signed a comprehensive accord in 2003.

Since the establishment of diplomatic relations between China and Korea in 1992, bilateral trade has seen rapid growth. Since then, the patterns of trade between China and Korea have dramatically changed. In 1992, the commodity trade volume between the two countries was around

US$ 6 billion per year, but it grew to $118 billion in 2006 (as shown in Figure III-1). More importantly, China's trade deficit with South Korea has increased with the increased trade volume between the two countries. China had a trade surplus with Korea in 1992, but it became a large deficit in 2000 and grew to about $23 billion in 2005.

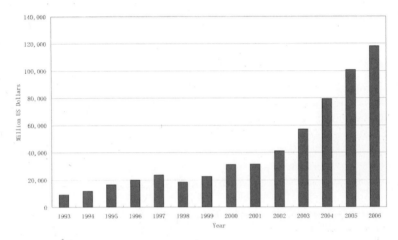

Source: KITA (Korea international trade associate)

Figure III-1 Trades between China and South Korea (Million US Dollars)

The trade value between Korea and China increased from US$ 6.4 billion in 1992 to US$ 118 billion in 2006, expanding 19-fold. During this period, Korea's exports and imports with China expanded 26-fold and 13-fold respectively. In 2006, Korea exported US$ 69.5 billion worth in goods to China and imported US$ 48.6 billion from China, realizing a trade surplus of US$ 20.9 billion. Korea's trade surplus has been widening in the past decade (from 1996 to 2006) with an accumulated surplus of US$ 111 billion. On the other hand, in 2006, Korea kept a trade deficit of US$ 25.4 billion with Japan and US$ 1.3 billion with Germany (See figure III-2).

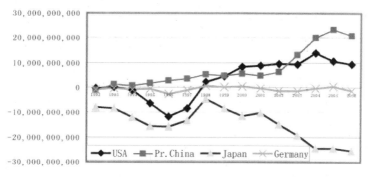

Source: KITA

Figure Ⅲ-2 Korea's Trade Balance with Its Major Trade Partners (US $)

The trade relations between Korea and China have been steadily progressing in terms of the share of bilateral trade, as a growing number of Korea's companies are engaged in trade processing and international segmentation of production with China. As is apparent from Table Ⅲ-3, China's share of Korea's foreign trade has increased from 4.03 percent in 1992 to 18.59 percent in 2006, turning China into Korea's largest trading partner.

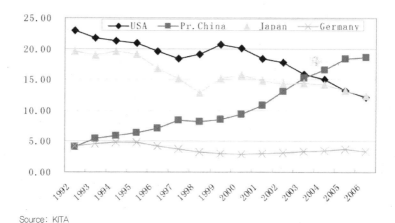

Source: KITA

Figure Ⅲ-3 Shares of Korea's Trade Partners in Its Foreign Trade (%)

CHAPTER 3. Economic Relations between China and Korea　73

However, during the same period the shares of the United States, Japan and Germany-currently the world's largest three economies-decreased from 22.96 percent, 19.61 percent, and 4.18 percent to 12.10 percent, 12.36 percent and 3.37 percent respectively. China is currently the largest buyer of Korea's products as well as the second largest seller to Korea closely following Japan. According to the data of Korea's import from China and Japan in 2006, I found a sharp increase rate for imports from China with 25.6 percent, compared to 7.3 percent from Japan of Korea's first buyer. Furthermore, the values of Korea's imports form China and Japan in 2006 are quite close, considering the different increase rate, we tend to predict that China will soon become Korea's biggest buyer and seller, as has been shown from the first two months' data in 2007. On the other hand, Korea's share of China's foreign trade also increased from 2 percent in 1990 to 8 percent in September 2005. Korea is now the third largest destination of China's exports and the second largest supplier of imports.

1.2. Trade Structures and Characteristics between China and Korea

The rapid integration of China into the global economy has posed particular problems for high income countries, including South Korea. China has a rapidly growing aggregate bilateral trade surplus with Korea, even according to Chinese data, and even when the miscounting of re-exports through Hong Kong are taken into account. Comparisons between sectoral trade volumes and trade surpluses can generate some interesting information necessary for understanding changes in the overall pattern of bilateral trade between two countries during the period 1994 to 2006. For many years, China's principal exports to South Korea focus on textile raw material, crude oil and finished product, corn, coal and other raw materials. Other large commodities include raw material for chemical industry, steel, leather products, footwear, feed-stuff and machinery and electric appliances. In recent years, high value-added products account more in exports to Korea, such as electronic parts. China principal imports from Korea include chemical product, electronic product, paper sheet, steel and etc.

Table Ⅲ-1 Changes in Korea's Export Structure by Commodities to China (SITC 1-digit)

Year	Major commodity shares in Korean exports to China (%)
1994	6(42%) > 7(23%) > 5(19%) > 2(5.6%) > 8(5%) > 3(4.7%) > 0(0.5%) > 9(0.0034%) > 1(0.0029%)
2000	7(31%) > 6(29%) > 5(22.3%) > 3(10%) > 8(4.9%) > 2(2.9%) > 0(0.67%) > 9(0.08%) > 1(0.03%)
2006	7(47%) > 5(18.9%) > 6(13.4%) > 8(11%) > 3(7.5%) > 2(1.4%) > 0(0.37%) > 9(0.1%) > 1(0.03%)

Source: Korea Trade Information Services (KOTIS), 2006. Author calculated depending on KOTIS database

Table Ⅲ-1 show changes in the Korean export structure to China by commodities from 1994 to 2006 based on the SITC 1-digit classification system. In 1994, the largest share of exports to China were 'manufactured goods' (42%) followed by 'machinery and transport equipment' (23%) and 'chemical products' (19%). The three groups accounted for a majority of the Korean export shares to China, about 84%. But in 2000, 'machinery and transport equipment' has ranked as the largest share (31%) of Korea's export to China while the shares of 'manufactured goods' has been decreased to 29%, followed by 'chemical products' with a little rising share(22.3%). Furthermore, in 2006, 'machinery and transport equipment' has not only continued to remain as the largest share of Korea's export to China, but secured a big rise (47%), almost accounting for half of the total of Korea's export to China.

Table Ⅲ-2 Changes in China's Export Structure by Commodities to Korea

Year	Major commodity shares in China's exports to Korea (%)
1994	6(33%) > 0(17%) > 3(14%) > 8(12%) > 2(8.6%) > 7(8%) > 5(7.6%) > 1(0.11%) > 4(0.1%)
2000	7(30%) > 6(22.6%) > 8(15%) > 0(12%) > 3(9%) > 5(6.5%) > 2(5%) > 1(0.038) > 4(0.0377)
2006	7(40%) > 6(26.6%) > 8(15%) > 5(6.5%) > 0(4.9%) > 3(4.5%) > 2(2.3%) > 1(0.05%) > 4(0.048%)

Source: KOTIS, 2006. Author calculated depending on KOTIS database

Table Ⅲ-2 presents changes in China's export structure to Korea in 1994, 2000, and 2006 respectively. In 1994, China's three major exporting commodities to Korea were 'manufactured goods' (33%), 'food and live animals' (17%) and 'mineral fuels, lubricants, and related materials' (14%). In 2000 and 2006, China's three major exporting commodities to Korea had found a new ranking in 'machinery and transport equipment' (30% in 2000 and 40% in 2006), 'manufactured goods' (22.6% in 2000 and 26.6% in 2006) and miscellaneous manufactured articles (15% in both 2000 and 2006).

Table Ⅲ-3 Trade between Korea and China in Different Industries

Trade (Million US$) Industries	1994		2000		2006	
	K-X	C-X	K-X	C-X	K- X	C- X
Food and live animals	31	916	123	1,532	258	2,394
Beverages and tobacco	0	6	5	5	23	24
Crude materials	348	472	535	624	986	1,137
Mineral fuels, lubricants	289	747	1,855	1,158	5,227	2,189

Animal and vegetable oils ,fats and waxes	0	5	4	5	6	23
Primary Industries	668	2146	2522	3324	6500	5767
Chemicals	1,181	415	4,114	830	13,088	3,165
Manufactured goods	2,610	1,797	5,274	2,888	9,546	12,894
Machinery and transport equipment	1,432	445	5,626	3,842	32,543	19,513
Miscellaneous manufactured articles	311	659	902	1,913	7,705	7,211
Commodities not classified	0	0	15	0.8	78	5.9
Labor intensive Industries	2,921	2,456	6,176	4,801	17,251	20,105
Capital or Tech Intensive Industries	2,613	860	9,755	4,673	45,709	22,684

Source: KOTIS. 2006. Author calculated depending on KOTIS database

To show more details capturing the main features of trade between China and Korea, I will categorize industries into three different groups by the SITC 1-digit code: A) Primary industries, which include food and live animals (0), beverage and tobacco (1), crude materials (2), mineral fuels and lubricants (3), animals and vegetable oils, fats and waxes; B) Labor intensive industries, which include manufactured goods (6) and Miscellaneous manufactured articles (8); C) Capital or technology-intensive industries, which include chemical (5), machinery and transport equipment (7), commodities, transactions not classified (9). Considering these classifications, I distract a good summary from Table III-3,

First, just as the huge increase of trade volume between China and Korea indicates, Table III-3 above illustrates the increasing and unequal bilateral trade volume in the primary, labor intensive industries and in capital and technology-intensive industries between Korea and China in 1994, 2000 and 2006. From the trade volumes among the three categories, it is evident that trade in each category between Korea and China from 1994 to 2006 has increased sharply. However, the trade volumes in primary industries, labor intensive industries and capital and technology-intensive industries have changed in different ways. Korea's export to China in the primary industries has increased from US$668 million in 1994 to US$6500 million in 2006, increasing 9.7-fold while China's export to Korea in primary industries just increased 2.7-folds during the same period, from US$2146 million to US$5767. This change reflects Korea's export in primary industries increased faster than Korean. In labor intensive industries, Korean exports to China increased 5.9 folds while China's exports to Korea increased 8.2-folds during the same time. This constellation reflects China's quick growth in these industries due to China's strong competitiveness in its cheap labor force. In capital or technology-intensive industries, Korean exports to China increased 17.5-folds from 1994 to 2006 and meanwhile China's exports to Korea increased 26.3-fold.

Table Ⅲ-4 Trade Shares between China and Korea in Industries from 1994 to 2006 (percent)

Trade Shares (%) Industry	1994 K-X	1994 C-X	2000 K-X	2000 C-X	2006 K-X	2006 C-X
0 Food and live animals	0.50	16.77	0.67	11.97	0.37	4.93
1 Beverages and tobacco	0.00	0.11	0.03	0.04	0.03	0.05
2 Crude materials	5.61	8.64	2.90	4.88	1.42	2.34
3 Mineral fuels, lubricants	4.66	13.68	10.05	9.05	7.53	4.51
4 Animal and vegetable oils, fats and waxes	0.00	0.09	0.02	0.04	0.01	0.05
Primary Industries	10.77	39.29	13.67	25.97	9.36	11.88
5 Chemicals	19.04	7.60	22.29	6.49	18.84	6.52
6 Manufactured goods	42.08	32.90	28.58	22.57	13.74	26.55
7 Machinery and transport equipment	23.09	8.15	30.49	30.02	46.85	40.19
8 Miscellaneous manufactured articles	5.01	12.07	4.89	14.95	11.09	14.85
9 Commodities not classified	0.00	0.00	0.08	0.01	0.11	0.01
Labor Intensive Industries	47.10	44.97	33.47	37.51	24.84	41.41
Capital(Tech) Intensive Industries	42.13	15.75	52.86	36.51	65.81	46.72

Source: KOTIS. 2006. Author calculated depending on KOTIS database

To find an overall picture of change in the export structure of China and Korea I first examine the sectoral distribution of their exports at the SITC1-digit level, using Korea International Trade Association (KOTIS) and United Nations trade statistics (UNCOMTRADE). From table III-4, we find that in 1994-2006 China, and Korea to a lesser extent, went through a major change in their export structure. In 1994, manufactured goods (SITC-6), mineral fuels (SITC-3), food and live animals (SITC-0), and crude material (SITC-2) accounted for close to 80 percent of China's exports to Korea, indicating that China's comparative advantage was then mainly in simple manufactured goods and raw materials. By 2006, however, China made a significant change in its export structure with machinery and transport equipment (SITC-7), miscellaneous manufactured articles (SITC-8), and manufactured goods (SITC-6) together accounting for 82 percent of its total exports to Korea. China was becoming rapidly industrialized, taking a significant leap in its export structure in only 13 years.

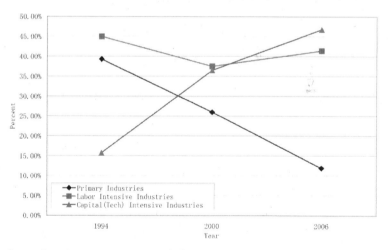

Source: Drawn by author depending on KOTIS

Figure III-4 China's Export Structures to Korea in 2006

Korea has also experienced changes in its export structure, albeit not as drastic as China. In 1994, three manufacturing sectors-SITC-7, SITC-8, and SITC-6-together accounted for 70.18 percent of Korea's exports to China, which means by 1994 Korea had become a highly industrialized economy. By 2006, the share of exports of SITC-8 and SITC-6 dropped significantly from 47.10 percent in 1994 to 24.84 percent in 2006, while the share of SITC-7 increased from23.09 to 46.85 percent. These are signs that Korea's comparative advantage has been shifting from low-wage, labor intensive to capital-intensive and technology-intensive manufacturing industries.

Next, the trading structures will be analyzed among the three categories for 2006. As figure Ⅲ-5 shows the differences of trade structures both in Korea and China reveal themselves more specifically. In 2006, the export of China to Korea ($5767 million) and Korea's export to China ($6500 million) in primary industries shared almost the same amounts.

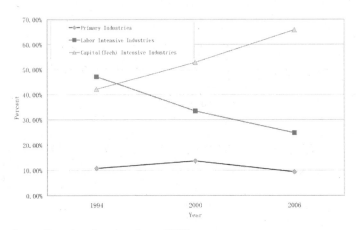

Source: Drawn by author depending on KOTIS

Figure Ⅲ-5 Korea's Export Structures to China in 2006

The Feasibility of a Korea-China FTA and its Potential Economic Effects

In labor intensive industries, China's export ($20 billion) was greater than Korea's ($17 billion), which coincides with China's labor force comparative advantage. However, in capital or technology industries, Korean exports ($45.7 billion) to China were two times greater than China's ($22.7 billion) export to Korea. Exports of Korean capital or technology industries accounted for 65.8% of Korea's total exports to China, while the export of China in capital intensive or high-tech industries just accounted for 46.7% of its total export to Korea. Thus I conclude export proportions between China and Korea to be quite close. But China's export proportions in labor-intensive industries are higher than Korea's while its export proportion in capital and high-tech intensive industries is lower than Korea's bilaterally. At this point, Korea's export structure is superior to China's.

Depending on more 2-digit SITC categories, the ten biggest trading sectors are checked between China and Korea in 2006. In terms of more narrowly defined two-digit SITC categories, Korea's four biggest exports to China were electrical machinery, apparatus, appliances (77, $12.3 billion), organic chemicals (51, $7.2 billion), office machines, automatic data processing machines(75, $6.1 billion), and telecommunication, sound--recording apparatuses (76, $5.8 billion), which account for the 45.2% of all of Korea's exports to China in 2006, which is shown in Table III-5. Among the ten sectors, Korea's export to China in industry seven accounted for a larger proportion (39.4%) (See table III-5).

Table Ⅲ-5 Korea's Ten Biggest Export Sectors to China in 2006

Table Ⅲ-5 Korea's Ten Biggest Export Sectors to China in 2006

Code	Commodity(Million US$)	Value	Shares
77	Electrical machinery, apparatus, appliances	12,314	17.7%
51	Organic chemicals	7,182	10.3%
75	Office machines, automatic data processing machines	6,125	8.8%
76	Telecommunication, sound recording apparatus	5,824	8.4%
87	Professional, scientific, controlling apparatus	5,194	7.5%
33	Petroleum, petroleum products	5,187	7.5%
57	Plastics in primary forms	4,093	5.9%
67	Iron and steel	3,184	4.6%
78	Road vehicles	3,158	4.5%
68	Non-ferrous metals	2,424	3.5%

Source: KOTIS, 2006. Author calculated depending on KOTIS database

Table Ⅲ-6 China's Ten Biggest Export Sectors to Korea in 2006

Code	Commodity(Million US$)	Value	shares
77	Electrical machinery, apparatus, appliances	9,465	19.5%
67	Iron and steel	5,437	11.2%
75	Office machines, automatic data processing machines	4,334	8.9%
76	Telecommunication, sound recording apparatus	2,969	6.1%
84	Articles of apparel and clothing accessories	2,922	6.0%
68	Non-ferrous metals	2,290	4.7%
65	Textile yarn ,fabrics, made-up articles	1,785	3.7%
69	Manufactures of metals	1,295	2.7%
32	Coal, coke and briquettes	1,260	2.6%
66	Non metallic mineral manufactures	1,231	2.5%

Source: KOTIS, 2006. Author calculated depending on KOTIS database

Table Ⅲ-6 lists China's ten biggest export sectors to Korea in 2006. As shown in the top panel, the industrial sector with the greatest dependence on exports to Korea was also industry seven which exported 34.5 percent of its total export to China. The first largest sector is electrical machinery, apparatus, and appliances (77, $9.5 billion). In turn, it was followed by iron and steel (67, $5.4 billion), office machines, automatic data processing machines (75, $4.3 billion) and telecommunication, sound-recording apparatus (76, $2.97 billion). From here, it probably can be concluded that China and Korea have a high intra-industry trade in industry seven (7, Machinery and transport equipment).

All in all, both Korea and China's trade structures have been upgraded since the establishment of formal relations between the two countries. During the adjustment of their industrial structures, they experienced differential growth periods. The structure of export commodities from China to Korea shows that China is now in a transition stage from resource and light textile industry to labor-intensive and heavy chemical industry, whereas Korea's export to China is changing from heavy chemical industry to high-tech industry. In the industrial "ranking" of world economies, Korea lies the stage ahead of China, which makes the economic relations between China and Korea more complementary than competitive. Such a situation will continue for a relatively long period and there will be huge potentials for further co-operation between China and Korea. Such a result supports the feasibility of a China-Korea FTA.

1.3. Deepening Investment Relations

Korean firms have entered the Chinese market through direct investment. Korea has become one of China's most important bilateral economic partners in terms of both trade and investment. Between 1990 and 2006, on average, the annual increase of the contracted and realized FDI amounts were 36.0 percent and 37.0 percent respectively, with realized FDIs reaching US$2.3 billion in 2006. In particular, Korea's FDI into China increased dramatically after the outbreak of the Korean Financial Crisis in 1997. Accordingly, the share of Korean FDI outflows has also increased steadily since 1999.

Lots of Korea's exports to China are raw materials, parts, and materials which are supplied to Korean firms that have set up operations in China. Although it was mostly South Korean small and medium-sized enterprises in labor-intensive industries that initially entered the Chinese market, major corporate groups such as Hyundai, Samsung and LG made their own advances beginning in the latter half of the 1990s. In line with such moves, South Korea's working population is shifting from the industrial sector to the service sector, namely the information sector. In this way, Korea is advancing its economy by transferring its gradually declining industries to China while focusing on nurturing new industries.

Since the breakout of the Financial Crisis in late 1997, Korean investment to China has seen a continuous decline. But since the waning of the crisis, newly signed Korean investment contracts to China increased dramatically. It is noteworthy that outflows of "contracted" FDIs into China have steadily risen since 1999, accompanying the recovery of the Korean economy. This suggests that Korean firms have been registering intent to invest in China in anticipation of stable investment environments that are likely to accompany China's entry into the WTO (See table III-7).

Table III-7 FDI Flows from Korea to China (US$ 1,000)

Year	Contracted		Realized	
	Project	Amount	Project	Amount
1990	39	55,624	24	16,174
1991	112	84,722	69	42,468
1992	269	223,113	170	141,127
1993	631	631,281	382	264,032

1994	1,065	825,141	840	635,847
1995	883	1,280,283	751	842,088
1996	927	1,958,961	740	930,154
1997	750	918,474	631	741,788
1998	318	905,073	266	696,066
1999	552	493,954	459	365,959
2000	910	990,033	775	712,068
2001	1,136	991,100	1,049	638,934
2002	1,544	2,045,637	1,389	1,032,112
2003	1,831	2,488,941	1,679	1,670,571
2004	2,243	3,522,378	2,143	2,300,675
2005	2,323	3,523,659	2,243	2,648,678
2006	2,290	4,516,895	2,303	3,319,751
2007 1-3	515	1,344,241	505	810,143
Total	18,352	26,812,680	16,426	17,815,005

Source: Korea Export Import Bank (2007)

Korea's FDI in China has shared such features as follow: First, the main feature of Korean FDI in China is that individual investment is relatively small and that most capital is concentrated in the labor-intensive industries (see table III-8 and figure III-6). Between 1996 and 2004, on average, the amount of individual Korean FDIs in China was US$0.96 million, which is substantially smaller than the average individual Korean FDI outflow into the world (US$2.86 million). During this period, about 42 percent of investments were conducted by small and medium-sized enterprises (SME). The size of individual investments ranged from a low of US$0.28 million in agriculture to a high of US$4.12 million in the communications industry and US$3.25 million in construction.[31] Although many of Korea's big companies, such as SK, LG and Samsung, have showed their interest in investing in China, the investment shares by

31) "Economic Effects of a Korea-China FTA and Policy Implications (I)"

SME are still dominant.

Table Ⅲ-8 Korea's FDI in China by Enterprise Size

	Cases				Amount(US$ 1,000)			
	Large	SME	Others	Total	Large	SME	Others	Total
1993	36	335	10	381	72,080	189,443	2,159	263,682
1994	91	706	44	841	343,435	283,986	6,475	633,896
1995	92	602	57	751	496,598	335,769	9,280	841,647
1996	75	489	173	737	579,307	307,945	24,528	911,780
1997	50	448	133	631	552,658	157,539	20,003	730,200
1998	20	174	68	262	597,888	85,559	8,060	691,507
1999	11	286	163	460	250,894	87,528	16,458	354,880
2000	14	561	200	775	480,805	180,474	24,848	686,127
2001	17	742	279	1,038	259,322	300,017	37,227	596,566
2002	35	937	403	1,375	417,592	511,261	70,284	999,137
2003	47	1,157	479	1,683	632,216	829,650	96,677	1,558,543
2004	72	1,097	984	2,153	833,915	1,185,521	197,575	2,217,011
Total	560	7,534	2,993	11,087	5,516,710	4,454,692	513,574	10,484,976
Ratio	5	68	27	100	52.6	42.5	4.9	100

Source: Korea Export Import Bank

Figure Ⅲ-6 the shares of Korea's FDI in China by Enterprise Size

Second, the majority of Korea's FDIs in China has entered manufacturing sectors defined as labor-intensive industries, some of which reflect relocation of manufacturing facilities from Korea to China. Between 1996 and 2004, FDIs in the manufacturing sector accounted for 85.2 percent of total FDIs. A large proportion of FDIs flowed into electrical and communication equipment, textiles, chemical and fuel products, and transport equipment. Between 1991 and 2004, electrical and communication equipment accounted for 25.3 percent of the total amount of FDIs, with textiles, chemical and fuel products, and transport equipment accounting for 12.2 percent, 10.9 percent, and 10.6 percent, respectively. In 2006, manufacturing accounted for 81.4 percent with wholesale, retail, and services accounting for 7.2 percent and 2.1 percent, respectively. On the other hand, investment areas have gradually been shifted from previously labor-intensive industries to capital or technology-intensive ones such as petrochemical industries, heavy industry, and automobiles and so on.

Table Ⅲ-9 Amount of Korea's FDI in China by Industry in 2006(US$ 1,000)

Sector	Contracted		Realized	
	Shares	Amount	Shares	Amount
Total		4,516,895	.	3,319,751
Agriculture & Fishery	0.5%	21,888	0.4%	12,977
Mining	0.5%	24,046	0.6%	19,331
Manufacturing	78.7%	3,554,328	81.4%	2,701,237
Construction	3.4%	152,663	2.1%	71,206
Whole sale & Retail	6.9%	312,610	7.2%	240,357
Transport & Storage	0.9%	38,755	0.3%	11,081
Telecommunications	0.0%	1,195	0.0%	681
Finance & Insurance	0.0%	0	0.0%	0
Lodging & Restaurants	1.2%	53,996	0.7%	23,396
Service	5.9%	267,361	5.1%	170,150
Real Estate	2.0%	90,053	2.1%	69,335
Others	0.0%	0	0.0%	0

Source: Korea Export Import Bank

Third-originally, the geographical distributions of Korea's investing projects were mainly concentrated in the coastal areas of eastern China, such as in Shandong, Jiangsu, Liaoning and Tianjing. Gradually these projects are expanding to other eastern areas like Guangdong and Fujian provinces, and the Koreans are also moving them to central and western provinces of China.

1.4. Trade Balance between China and Korea

Table Ⅲ-10 the Trade Balance between China and Korea from 1993 to 2007

Year	Korea's Export	China's Export	China's Deficit	China Deficit's Increase Rate
1994	6,203	5,463	740	135.4%
1995	9,144	7,401	1,742	62.9%
1996	11,377	8,539	2,838	21.7%
1997	13,572	10,117	3,456	58.0%
1998	11,944	6,484	5,460	-11.8%
1999	13,685	8,867	4,818	17.4%
2000	18,455	12,799	5,656	-13.6%
2001	18,190	13,303	4,888	30.0%
2002	23,754	17,400	6,354	107.8%
2003	35,110	21,909	13,201	52.9%
2004	49,763	29,585	20,178	15.3%
2005	61,915	38,648	23,267	-10.2%
2006	69,459	48,557	20,903	-74.8%
Apr-07	24792	19525	5267	

Source: KOTIS, 2006. (Million$)

From Table Ⅲ-10, I illustrate that since 1994, South Korea's trade surplus with China had risen by 28.2-fold to 20.9 billion US dollars in 2006. During this period, China's trade deficit with Korea had almost kept increasing. Although China's deficit increase rate seemed to decrease since 2004, deficit amounts continue to rise. Trade imbalance has become an important issue influencing the trade development in the future. It is necessary to conduct research that reveals the main reasons for this development to analyze the potential impact by the Korea-China FTA on trade balances between them.

As table III-11 shows, Korea's trade balance in primary industries has been improving from a trade deficit in 1994 (US$-1480 million) to a trade surplus in 2006(US$733 million). On the other hand, Korea's trade surplus in the manufacturing industry has been widening from US$1755 million in 1994 to US$23120 million in 2006, thus increasing more than five-fold. Among the manufacturing industries, machinery and transport equipment, office and automatic data processing machines, telecommunications equipment, electrical appliances, and road vehicles showed a significant increase in exports. Chemical products are also a significant source of Korea's trade surplus with China, representing 20.3 percent of the total surplus. In contrast, labor-intensive manufactured goods are facing a downturn, resulting in a trade deficit in 2006(US$ -2854 million). Thus a majority of trade imbalances occurred in capital or tech-intensive industries where China suffered a large deficit, reaching US$ 15800 million in 2006. This trade pattern reflects the fact that Korea tends to export intermediate and capital goods to China, which are used not only for the domestic consumption market but also for export-generating activities.

Table Ⅲ-11 Trade Balance between China and Korea in Different Industries

	Trade Surplus		
Year	1994	2000	2006
Food and live animals	-885	-1,409	-2,136
Beverages and tobacco	-6	0	-1
Crude materials, inedible, except fuels	-124	-89	-151·
Mineral fuels, lubricants and related materials	-458	697	3,038
Animal and vegetable oils ,fats and waxes	-5	-1	-17
Total Surplus of Primary Industries	-1478	-802	733
Chemicals	766	3,284	9,923
Manufactured goods	813	2,386	-3,348
Machinery and transport equipment	987	1,784	13,030
Miscellaneous manufactured articles	-348	-1,011	494
Commodities, transactions not classified	-747	-1,898	-7133
Total Surplus of Manufacturing Industries	1471	4,545	12,966
Labor intensive Industries	465	1375	-2854
Capital or Tech Intensive Industries	1006	3170	15820

Source: KOTIS. 2006. (Million$)

Based on the SITC 2-digit, table Ⅲ-12 shows that China's largest trade deficit with Korea are organic chemicals (SIC51), which is not surprising since Korea has always kept a comparative advantage in its chemicals with China. The next largest deficit is in professional, scientific, controlling apparatuses (SIC87), which are high-tech industries by most measures. Other commodity groups that also generated top trade deficits include petroleum, petroleum products (SIC33), plastics in primary forms (SIC57), telecommunication, and sound-recording apparatuses (SIC76). Electrical machinery, apparatus, appliances (SIC77), road vehicles (SIC78), and machinery specialize for particular industries (SIC72) along with office machines, automatic data processing machines (SIC75), and metalworking machinery (SIC73).

Table Ⅲ-12 China's Top ten Trade Deficit Groups with Korea in 2006

Code	Groups	China's Deficit	Deficit shares
51	Organic chemicals	-6003	17.6%
87	Professional, scientific, controlling apparatus	-4428	12.9%
33	Petroleum, petroleum products	-4272	12.5%
57	Plastics in primary forms	-3847	11.2%
76	Telecommunication, sound recording apparatus	-2855	8.3%
77	Electrical machinery, apparatus, appliances	-2849	8.3%
78	Road vehicles	-2713	7.9%
72	Machinery specialize for particular industries	-2029	5.9%
75	Office machines, automatic data processing machines	-1791	5.2%
73	Metalworking machinery	-596	1.7%
	Total Deficit in 2006	-20,903	

Source: Korea KITA, Korea trade statistics

Taken together, machinery and transport equipment (SIC7) trade is responsible for 37 percent of China's total trade deficit with Korea. Industries 5 and 7 are defined as high-technology category. Only one of the top ten trade deficit groups is what economists traditionally consider to be low-technology products (petroleum, petroleum products 33). China's trade deficit mainly involve high-technology and high-wage production industries, which indicates that Korea's export to China has a comparative technological advantage and the difference of the technology works as a significant cause of China's trade deficit with Korea. China's overall trade deficit with Korea in these ten industries was $31 billion in 2006, which exceeds the total Korean deficit with China in that year by a substantial amount. If the deficit in those ten industries could be eliminated, then the trade deficit could be converted into a 10.4 billion surplus.

1.5 Trade Policy

With regard to their overall average applied tariff levels, China and Korea showed similar figures in 2006, with China's overall tariff level being 9.9% and Korea's 11.9%. In sector level, China's average tariff rate was 15.2% for agricultural products and 8.95% for industrial goods in 2006, while Korea's averages were 41.5% for agricultural products and 6.7% for industrial goods. In other words, Korea imposes relatively high levels of tariffs on agricultural products compared to those on industrial goods. On the other hand, China's average tariff rate for manufactured products, especially heavy-industrial products, is slightly higher than that of Korea. Korea implements an adjustment tariff scheme (ATS) which is consistent with the WTO Agreement, as it operates within the scope of Korea's WTO bound rates and on an MFN basis. The ATS is designed to prevent disruption of the domestic market or collapse of the relevant industries, while it applies to agricultural and non-agricultural products. Both China and Korea are active participants in the multilateral trading regime. Korea has been a member of WTO since the organization's establishment in 1995, and China became a WTO member in 2001. The two countries are committed to multilateral trade liberalization under the agent of the WTO. Both China and Korea are working hard with other WTO members to push the Doha Development Agenda and Doha Round of trade negotiations, which was launched in 2001, forward to a successful conclusion.

■ China' Trade and Investment Policy

Trade promotion

Chinese government takes full-round measures to help Chinese enterprise, especially the SMEs involved in foreign trade. Providing all kinds information channel, such as export / import Commodities Fair, to assist the Chinese enterprises in developing international market and in facilitating the Chinese enterprises' exchanges and cooperation with the other countries' companies. Providing the enterprises with the information on trade partner countries' economic environment and the foreign enterprises' credit situation; establishing and maintaining foreign trade enterprise credit system.

Organizing import and export related trainings and the seminars on trade remedy; Helping Chinese enterprises to respond to the trade remedy investigations initiated by foreign governments. The China Council for the Promotion of International Trade (CCPIT) is the most important and the largest institution for the promotion of foreign trade in China. It comprises individuals, enterprises and organizations representing the economic and trade sectors in China.

Investment promotion

China encourages inflow and outflow of FDI. The Investment Promotion Agency of the Ministry of Commerce, P.R.C. (CIPA) and China Council for International Investment Promotion are the important institutions for the promotion of investment both in China and abroad. Many provinces provide one-stop shop services to foreign investors, and have set up investment complaint service centers. Each province has set up an investment promotion centre. China also promotes investment through the International Fair for

Investment and Trade, China Central Expo, etc. China has also established bilateral investment promotion agencies with other countries and regions in the world to promote bilateral investment.

For promoting trade and investment, Chinese government has continued to adopt measures to increase the level of transparency of its trade and investment policies, practices, and measures. All information related to FDI, foreign trade-related laws, regulations, and rules are published in the China Foreign Trade and Economic Gazette, which is edited and published by MOFCOM. Enquiry points and enquiry websites are set up by MOFCOM and the General Administration of Quality Supervision, Inspection and Quarantine (AQSIQ) and China makes regular notifications to the WTO. Newly promulgated trade-related laws and regulations are compiled and published by the Legislative Affairs Office of the State Council, which also publishes the yearly collection of China's laws and regulations governing foreign- related matters.

■ Korea's Trade and Investment Policy

Trade Pomotion

Korean trade policy in general and free trade policy in particular has traditionally been focused on multilateral negotiations and dispute resolution mechanisms. South Korea has been consistently advocating that an open and strong multilateral trading system is fundamental to economic growth and development. In parallel with these efforts for trade liberalization on the multilateral front, Korea has been making efforts to deepen mutually beneficial bilateral trade relations with its trading partners. As part of these efforts, Korea has been engaged in several WTO-consistent regional FTA.

To Korea, the objective of pursuing FTAs is to manage its bilateral trade relations in a more systematic manner and secure better access in trade and investment to foreign markets which may be unavailable under the multilateral setting. The implement of FTAs will prompt the domestic restructuring of less competitive sectors and thus raise the level of efficiency within the economy. In this light, Korea believes that these FTAs will complement, not replace, efforts for multilateral trade liberalization. FTAs not only result in trade liberalization but can also lead to substantial improvement in the domestic regulatory framework. More importantly, benefits from certain reform measures brought about by FTAs can be shared by all countries, not just by the FTA partners, as negotiations in such areas as competition, services, and customs procedures often relate to the regulatory framework.

Investment Promotion

Since the onset of the financial crisis in 1997, the Korean government has been active in its efforts to attract foreign direct investment to Korea, which was facilitated by the enactment of the Foreign Investment Promotion. The Korean government selected green growth sectors and 17 growth engine industries across the economy to focus its support, and expand their competitiveness to further promote foreign investment. To concentrate government-wide efforts for FDI promotion, the government has also adopted an accountability system where every ministry is held accountable. In addition, the government organized a high-level team to improve the foreign investment environment to resolve investment-related grievances on the ground, and took various measures to develop free economic zones, from deregulation on development procedures, building infrastructure to land development.

The government currently offers tax relief to foreign companies with the potential to make major contributions to the Korean economy, provides them with industrial sites or assists them with site location and acquisition, and provides cash grants and other types of financial support. Starting from 2009, foreign investment with the potential to create jobs, and high-degree technology businesses, has become eligible for cash grants. Beneficiaries of rent reduction were expanded to include foreign investment zones exclusively reserved for parts and materials companies. Foreign investors may receive financial support from provincial governments for expansion or establishment of International schools under local government ordinances.

Foreign companies in industry support services or high-degree technology businesses specified by the Ministry of Strategy and Finance, or foreign investment in manufacturing, logistics, R&D, and leisure & hotel businesses based in foreign investment zones or free economic zones are eligible for tax relief on corporate, income, local, and dividend income taxes for five to seven years. Customs duty reduction or exemption is also available on capital goods whose import declaration is completed within three years from the date of investment notification. Prospective investors may advance notice on whether their line of business is eligible for the current tax relief program and the extent of the tax benefits they will receive so that they can make an informed decision. In additon to tax breaks on FDI, investors may benefit from various incentive programs such as investment tax credit and SME tax support.

02 | A Competitiveness and Complementariness Research of Korea and China's Industries

World trade relationships are changing rapidly. Regional trade arrangements proliferate even with considerable progress in multilateral trade liberalization. Without any institutional framework on bilateral integration, however, China and Korea have been experiencing significant changes and progress in their economic relationships in trade, especially during the last two decades or so. The purpose of this thesis section is to examine the trade competitiveness structure of the two Northeast Asian countries, in terms of the "Revealed Comparative Advantage" (RCA) index. I will also analyze the two countries' trade complementariness through the "Intra Industry Trade" (IIT) index so as to estimate trade status and directions of trade between them. Depending on my findings, I will illustrate the two countries' bilateral trading structures, trading advantages, and the technology content of the trading products to analyze the rationales of a Korea-China FTA.

2.1. An Analysis of RCA Index

In order to look at the trade relationship between Korea and China in a constructive way, market share analysis will be conducted through RCA and IIT based on major commodities. The analyses will help anticipate competitive or complementary exports of goods for a Korea-China FTA by commodity levels if a Korea-China FTA is successfully concluded. Market Share Analysis and a RCA analysis present very different pictures for competitiveness among exports. The IIT index will help project the benefits of a Korea-China FTA. I investigate the trends and characteristics of the China-Korea bilateral trade.

More than 40 years ago, Bela Balassa published a paper[32] for the first time using the measure of 'Revealed Comparative Advantage' (RCA). Since then the measure has been applied in numerous reports[33] and academic publications[34] as a way to evaluate international trade specialization. RCA analysis is used to help understand a country's comparative trade advantage. Competitiveness of each country's export goods is observed by measuring its RCA index. Actually, there are many different methods for the application of the RCA index. The first RCA index used here was defined by Balassa and the second is made up of RCAx and RCAm based on a formula by Das.[35] Balassa's RCA index will firstly be used to analyze the bilateral trading relationship as formula (1),

$$RCA_{ij} = \frac{X_{ij} \Big/ \sum_i X_{ij}}{\sum_j X_{ij} \Big/ \sum_i \sum_j X_{ij}}, \tag{1}$$

Where X_{ij} : Country i's exports of sector j to the world

         $\sum_i X_{ij}$: Country i's total exports

         $\sum_j X_{ij}$: Total world exports of sector j

         $\sum_i \sum_j X_{ij}$: Total world exports

The numerator represents the percentage shares of a given sector in national exports-Xij are exports of sector i from country j. The denominator represents the percentage share of a given sector in world exports. The RCA index, thus, contains a comparison of a national export structure

---

32) Balassa, Bela, 1965.

33) UNIDO, 1986 and World Bank, 1994.

34) For example, in Aquino, (1981); Crafts and Thomas, (1986); van Hulst et al, (1991); Lim, (1997).

35) Das (1998).

(the numerator) with a world export structure (the denominator). When RCA equals 1 for a given sector in a given country, the percentage share of that sector is identical with the world average. When RCA Bersa when RCA is below 1.

As shown above, the RCA index is defined as the share of each commodity group in an economy's total exports divided by that commodity group's share of world exports. The more this index is above 1, the stronger is that economy's comparative advantage in that commodity group, which means if the calculated RCA in k product is larger than one, the country has a comparative advantage in it.

Table Ⅲ-13 Korea's RCA index to the world by commodity from 2002 to 2005

	Korea RCA	2002	2003	2004	2005
0&1	Food and live animals, beverages and tobacco	0.23	0.20	0.19	0.18
2&4	Crude materials, animal, vegetable oils, fats and waxes	0.29	0.29	0.27	0.28
3	Mineral fuels, lubricants and related materials	0.42	0.35	0.37	0.40
5	Chemicals	0.79	0.79	0.83	0.91
7	Machinery and transport equipment	1.50	1.56	1.59	1.59
6&8	manufactured goods	0.86	0.83	0.78	0.85

Source: Author's calculation based on UN Comtrade data and its Yearbook 2005

The above table Ⅲ-13 shows Korea's RCA index from 2002 to 2005 depending on the SITC 1-digit. Here, Korea appears to have comparative advantage in machinery and transport equipment whose RCA index is always greater than 1 from 2002 to 2005. Besides, Korea's chemicals and manufactured goods also show relatively high comparative advantage with an RCA index of 0.91 and 0.85, respectively in 2005.

Table Ⅲ-14 China's RCA index to the world by commodity from2002 to 2005

	China's RCA	2002	2003	2004	2005
0&1	Food and live animals, beverages and tobacco	0.70	0.63	0.54	0.52
2&4	Crude materials, animal, vegetable oils, fats and waxes	0.39	0.32	0.27	0.28
3	Mineral fuels, lubricants and related materials	0.27	0.25	0.22	0.17
5	Chemicals (capital intensive)	0.45	0.41	0.41	0.44
7	Machinery and transport equipment(capital)	0.87	0.98	1.05	1.11
6&8	Manufactured goods (labor intensive)	1.90	1.82	1.78	1.82

Source: Author's calculation based on UN Comtrade data and its Yearbook 2005

On the other hand, table Ⅲ-14 implies that China's RCA index in a global context indicates a relative competitiveness in machinery, transport equipment and manufactured goods. According to the SITC rules, the groups from 0 to 4 generally indicate primary commodities while groups 6 and 8 indicate labor-intensive manufactured goods. Groups 5 and 7 relate to capital or technology-intensive manufactured goods. From the evolution of a time series, we can see the comparative advantage in China's primary industries has been decreased. However, while China kept its strong competition in its traditional manufactured goods, China has improved its comparative advantage in its capital or technology-intensive industries, and the improvement of its machinery and transport equipment is just a good example.

Table Ⅲ-15 The Comparison of Korea and China's RCA in 1997

The Comparison of Korea and China's RCA		1997	
Code	Industries	Korea RCA	China RCA
0	Food and live animals	0.28	0.93
1	Beverages and tobacco	0.09	0.53
2	Crude materials, inedible, except fuels	0.39	0.64
3	Mineral fuels, lubricants	0.41	0.51
4	Animal and vegetable oils, fats and waxes	0.04	0.77

5	Chemicals	0.80	0.62
6	Manufactured goods	1.22	1.28
7	Machinery and transport equipment	1.15	0.61
8	Miscellaneous manufactured articles	0.65	2.96

Source: Wu Xiang (2004)

In the past, China has always been known to be most competitive in labor intensive industries, which can also explain why China's manufactured goods are so competitive in the world. However, it is really surprising to notify that China nowadays has a strong comparative advantage in high value-added or capital-intensive industries like machinery and manufactured goods.

Compared table Ⅲ-13, Ⅲ-14 and Ⅲ-15, the variations of the RCA index by industry both in Korea and in China can be inferred. First, the RCA index of manufactured goods between Korea and China were almost same in 1997, with Korea's RCA index 1.22 and China's 1.28. But Korea's RCA index of manufactured goods decreased to 0.85 while China's RCA index of manufactured goods increased to 1.82 in 2005. Such a shift is partly due to Korea's growing direct investment in China. More and more Korea's companies have been investing in China with the intention of making full use of China's cheap labor force to reduce its product costs while exporting their products from China to the whole world. To this point, it is Korea-invested companies in China which help to promote the competition of China's manufactured goods. Such a tendency implies China's labor-intensive advantage is still competitive in the world because of its natural advantage from abundantly cheap work forces.

Second, in 1997, Korea's RCA index in machinery and transport equipment was much greater than that of China. But in 2005, Korea's RCA index in machinery and transport equipment decreased to 0.82 from 1.15 in 1997 and China's increased to 1.11 from 0.61 in 1997. Applying the RCA index in 2005, we find the comparative advantage in China's manufactured goods: machinery and transport equipment have greatly increased from 1997 to 2005 while Korea's comparative advantages decreased in these industries during this period, which means that China's export structure improved. My RCA data reflects China's RCA indices in its primary industries have decreased. China's RCA dropped off in groups 0, 1, 2, 3, 4 and its group 3's RCA dwindled from 0.51 in 1997 to 0.17 in 2005 with a sharp downturn. During this period China's capital or technology-intensive industries, such as groups 6, 7, and 8 have greatly enhanced their competitiveness in the world. While from another perspective, just as what Korean companies have done in China, the competition promotion of foreign-invested companies in China contributed much to China's export enhancement and advancement. At present, foreign-invested enterprises have accounted for half of China's total exports. In 2005, foreign-invested enterprises accounted for 58.3 percent of China's total exports. Among the commodities with high technology, the export proportion of foreign-invested enterprises in China's total exports surpasses 85 percent.

Third, we find Korean capital or technique industries still own comparative advantages compared to China. China's comparative advantage index in chemical industry has decreased from 0.62 in 1997 to 0.44 in 2005 while Korea's RCA index in chemical industry continued increasing from 0.80 in 1997 to 0.91 in 2005. Furthermore, Korea's machinery and transport equipment has also been keeping an increasing tendency from 1.50 in 2002 to 1.59 in 2005, which is greater than China's with a RCA 1.11 of same industry in 2005.

However, since the RCA turns out to produce an output which cannot be compared on both sides of 1, the index is made symmetric, obtaining 1 as (RCA-1)/ (RCA+1). This measure ranges from -1 to +1. The measure is labeled 'Revealed Symmetric Comparative Advantage' (RSCA). According to Laursen's research, RSCA is the best measure of comparative advantage compared to RCA, to CTB measures and to the Michaely index. I decided to use RSCA to test the trade specialization of both Korea and China. From Table III-16 using the RSCA index, Korea also shows an apparent comparative advantage in its chemical industries within the world market. China's manufactured goods have a relative comparative advantage. All results are consistent with RCA indices.

Table III-16 Korea and China's RSCA from 2002 to 2005

	Korea				China			
	2002	2003	2004	2005	2002	2003	2004	2005
0&1	-0.63	-0.66	-0.69	-0.70	-0.17	-0.23	-0.30	-0.32
2&4	-0.55	-0.55	-0.58	-0.56	-0.44	-0.52	-0.58	-0.56
3	-0.41	-0.48	-0.46	-0.42	-0.57	-0.60	-0.64	-0.71
5	-0.12	-0.12	-0.10	-0.05	-0.38	-0.42	-0.42	-0.39
7	0.20	0.22	0.23	0.23	-0.07	-0.01	0.02	0.05
6&8	-0.07	-0.09	-0.12	-0.08	0.31	0.29	0.28	0.29

Source: Author's calculation based on UN Comtrade data and its Yearbook 2005

In order to discover the comparative advantage between Korea and China, the traditional Balassa RCA index and RSCA are not enough, because they just reflect the two countries' comparative levels world wide. Some industries, probably both in Korea and China lack competition in a world scope, but Korea or China may have a comparative advantage on bilateral levels. Therefore, other measures need to be resorted in order to make sense of a more specific analysis in bilateral-trading structures between Korea and China. The RCAx and RCAm index was developed by Das (1998) which is well utilized to analyze the bilateral trading structures and bilateral trading competition. The two indices are defined as follows:

$$RCAx = (Xi/X)/(Wix/Wx), \qquad (2)$$

Where Xi: Country A's exports to country B of product k

               X: Country A's total exports to country B

               Wix: Country A's world exports of product k

               Wx: Country A's total world exports

$$RCAm = (Mi/M)/(Wim/Wm), \qquad (3)$$

Where Mi: Country A's imports from country B of product k

               M: Country A's total imports from country B

               Wim: Country A's world imports of product k

               Wm: Country A's total world imports

Table III-17 China's RCAx and RCAm Indices to Korea

	China's RCAx Index						China's RCAm Index					
Y	2000	2001	2002	2003	2004	2005	2000	2001	2002	2003	2004	2005
0	2.48	2.27	2.56	2.81	2.11	2.44	0.22	0.2	0.19	0.2	0.17	0.2
1	0.18	0.42	0.28	0.46	0.43	0.52	0.04	0.05	0.1	0.09	0.16	0.13
2	2.42	2.17	2.15	2.15	1.98	2.49	0.31	0.24	0.22	0.17	0.12	0.11

3	2.72	3.05	2.81	2.63	2.54	2.84	0.93	1.12	0.68	0.6	0.57	0.46
4	0.85	1.45	1.23	1.96	2.08	1.7	0.04	0.04	0.02	0.02	0.01	0.01
5	1.42	1.39	1.4	1.43	1.35	1.39	1.64	1.67	1.52	1.39	1.42	1.42
6	1.52	1.33	1.39	1.43	1.53	1.64	1.71	1.76	1.45	1.3	1.29	1.21
7	0.82	0.84	0.76	0.74	0.8	0.79	0.74	0.72	0.91	0.95	0.97	1.05
8	0.45	0.55	0.63	0.66	0.66	0.55	0.74	0.8	1	1.52	1.74	1.68
9	0.08	0.04	0.01	0.21	0.16	0.19	0.05	0.07	0.15	1.04	0.53	0.28

Source: KOTIS, 2006. Author calculated depending on KOTIS database

Table Ⅲ-18 Korea's RCAx and RCAm Indices to China

	Korea's RCAx Index						Korea's RCAm Index					
	2000	2001	2002	2003	2004	2005	2000	2001	2002	2003	2004	2005
0	0.17	0.12	0.10	0.10	0.12	0.11	2.96	2.17	2.17	2.25	1.57	1.74
1	0.08	0.09	0.10	0.11	0.16	0.15	0.12	0.15	0.14	0.26	0.30	0.28
2	0.47	0.36	0.32	0.29	0.24	0.24	0.80	0.57	0.51	0.47	0.38	0.45
3	0.42	0.39	0.25	0.25	0.25	0.21	0.38	0.40	0.40	0.34	0.32	0.24
4	0.13	0.10	0.09	0.07	0.04	0.03	0.21	0.16	0.19	0.24	0.18	0.27
5	2.71	2.51	2.24	1.97	2.05	1.99	0.79	0.78	0.68	0.67	0.67	0.67
6	2.47	2.34	1.79	1.62	1.25	1.10	1.95	1.65	1.58	1.56	1.79	1.85
7	0.83	0.94	1.25	1.39	1.45	1.53	0.82	0.95	0.93	1.01	1.11	1.22
8	0.67	0.66	0.56	0.60	0.88	1.22	2.04	2.16	2.13	2.03	1.80	1.59
9	0.05	0.09	0.09	0.07	0.08	0.21	0.00	0.00	0.02	0.04	0.10	0.06

Source: KOTIS, 2006. Author calculated depending on KOTIS database

Speaking depending on the indices, China appears to be more competitive in commodity groups 0, 2, 3, 4 such as food, crude materials, and vegetables and so on, which are mostly labor-intensive industries. It also turns out that Korea is strongly competitive in relative capital-intensive industries like chemicals reflected by commodity group five. Korea's group seven also behaves a little less comparative compared to China's advantage. From the trade shares of the two countries' competitive advantage commodity from 2000 to 2005, Korea and China's shares of their competitive commodity trading values are almost the same. In 2005, China's shares of competitive advantage commodity accounted for 10% of its entire trade value with Korea and Korea accounts for about 14% (here I define group five as Korean comparative advantage commodity). If Korean competitive industries include not only group 5 but group 7, the Korean competitive commodity trading shares will be 66.5 % and 66% in 2005 and 2006, respectively. Such a trade structure probably partly explains why there is a huge deficit for China's trade balance compared to Korea (See table III-17 and III-18). China's recent, fast-rising competitiveness in manufacturing reflects the acceleration and improvement in manufactured goods. It is worthwhile to note that the rising competitive advantage of China's industries may reflect the comfort and ease of foreign-invested companies to operate in fast-developing China today.

Therefore, compared to Balassa's RCA and RSCA indices, the same results appear from the bilateral RCAx and RCAm indices. From here, I conclude that both Korea and China's trading structures are highly complementary and their respective comparative advantages are not apparent. Especially the shares of their comparative advantage commodities behave without much variation. Considering the huge trade volume between them, it appears the majority of trade volume between the two countries may happen in an intra-industry pattern. As a result, an intra-industry trade analysis between them is made in the next part.

2.2. Technological Classifications of Exports

To find an answer to the question of what has brought the change about in the export structure, products are grouped in terms of production technology. That is, following Lall,[36] the products classified at the 3-digit SITC level are divided into ten subgroups divided in terms of the level of production technology. It follows in two steps: products are first divided into five groups-primary products (PP), resource-based products (RB), low-technology products (LT), medium-technology products (MT), and high technology products (HT). The latter four are further divided into agriculture-based products (RB1), other resource-based products (RB2), textile/fashion cluster (LT1), other low technology products (LT2), automotive products (MT1), process industries-chemical and basic metals-(MT2), engineering products (MT3), electronics and electrical products (HT1), and other high-technology products (HT2) (see table III-19).

Table III-19 Technological Classification of Exports

	PP	RB1	RB2	LT1	LT2	MT1	MT2	MT3	HT1	HT2
China										
1991	18.1	4.44	5.82	31.35	11.42	6.74	5.08	10.13	4.09	1.64
1996	9.99	5.24	5.59	30.18	15.52	0.94	5.94	11.17	12.59	2.34
2001	6.92	3.86	5.03	24.71	14.96	1.55	5.06	13.22	21.84	2.15
Korea										
1991	3.21	3.19	4.24	22.82	11.57	3.67	12.39	16.77	20.25	1.26
1996	2.38	3.45	5.41	10.76	8.22	8.98	12.58	16.09	26.7	1.08
2001	2.27	3.19	8.18	9.22	7.44	10.2	9.87	17.6	30.04	1.04

As aforementioned, China has rapidly increased its exports of electronics and other electrical products. Although they are classified as high-technology products, the nature of technology associated with their production in China is quite varied. While some of them require advanced technology and extensive R&D, others involve only simple labor-intensive processes.

---

36) Lall (2000)

Furthermore, many of these products are only assembled at foreign-owned or joint venture enterprises that are in China mainly to take advantage of its low-cost labor.[37] At present, China may be able to export these products only with the help of foreign investors, but that does not mean this situation will remain so for long. Given that foreign direct investment has enabled rapid catching-up industrialization in other parts of Asia,[38] there is no reason why China will not be able to do the same and replicate the catch-up development achieved by Japan and the Asian NIEs. In the case of Korea, the most dramatic increase took place in export shares of electronics and electrical products (HT1), albeit not as much as in China. Unlike the case of China, this increase is from Korea's indigenous firms, an indication that they have acquired their own capability for producing high technology products. Also, as to be expected, the export share of textiles (LT1) and other labor-intensive products (LT2) decreased from a combined share of 43 percent to a little over 16 percent.[39]

2.3. The Intra-Industry Trade Analysis between Korea and China

Intraregional industry trade is always one of the major issues when the impact and political feasibility of a FTA is discussed. Traditional trade theory such as that of Heckscher-Ohlin well explains 'inter-industry trade' based on comparative advantage in economic terms. Different from the theory of comparative advantage, the real world has a trade pattern

---

37) Fung and Iizaka, 2002.

38) Yamazawa, 1990.

39) Joon-Kyung Kim, Yangseon Kim and Chung H. Lee (2004).

of "intra-industry" in considerable amounts. To explain the intra-industry trade pattern, some assumptions are used such as the economies of scale and imperfect competition. The Grubel-Lloyd Index is used to analyze the intra-industry trade pattern between Korea and China. In this session, I construct a Grubel-Lloyd index of intra-industry trade (IIT). Krugman argues that economics of scale arising from intra-industry trade are thought to lead to more rapid productivity gains and hence faster growth. The index is defined as:

$$IITi \ = \ 1 \ - \ \mid Xi \ - \ Mi \mid /(Xi \ + \ Mi), \hspace{2cm} (4)$$

Where, Xi: Korea's export of commodity i to China
Mi: Korea's import of commodity i from China.

The formula above is for intra-industry trade in commodity i, and the following formula is for the intra-industry trade in all industries.

$$IIT \ = \ 1 \ - \ \Sigma i \mid Xi \ - \ Mi \mid /\Sigma i(Xi \ + \ a \ Mi), \hspace{1.5cm} (5)$$

The IIT index ranges between zero and one, with larger values indicating a greater level of trade between firms in the same industry. Higher IIT ratios suggest that net gains from specialization in different products should be exploited and that the participating country should increase its integration into the world economy. The GL ratio (or IIT ratio) ranges between 0 and 1: when it is close to 1, intra-industry trade is active, and vice versa.

In order to capture how intra-industry trade varies between countries, the intra-industry trade indices were calculated between China and Korea over the period of 2000 to 2006, the data of which is presented in table Ⅲ-20. It shows that IIT indices between Korea and China turn out to be greater than 0.5 in most cases. The industries of beverages and tobacco, crude materials, mineral fuels, lubricants and related materials, manufactured goods and machinery and transport equipment exhibit highest level of intra-industry trade. The IIT index for manufactured goods has risen from 0.71 in 2000 to 0.97 in 2005 and 0.85 in 2006, while the IIT indexes for animal and vegetable oils, fats and waxes have substantially decreased in this period. So the intra-industry trade and structures between the two countries has supplied a good background and basis for the formation of CK FTA. In this sense, CK FTA will significantly and positively lead to economic growth in both countries.

Table Ⅲ-20 Intra-Industry Trade between China and Korea

	2000	2001	2002	2003	2004	2005	2006
0	0.15	0.14	0.12	0.14	0.24	0.19	0.19
1	0.99	0.89	0.98	0.83	0.95	0.91	0.97
2	0.92	0.92	0.93	1.00	0.97	0.92	0.93
3	0.77	0.86	0.92	0.93	0.86	0.82	0.59
4	0.93	0.89	0.77	0.65	0.57	0.30	0.39
5	0.34	0.37	0.36	0.35	0.32	0.35	0.39
6	0.71	0.68	0.79	0.75	0.92	0.97	0.85
7	0.81	0.85	0.70	0.62	0.63	0.67	0.75
8	0.64	0.59	0.53	0.64	0.91	0.90	0.97
9	0.10	0.08	0.24	0.55	0.88	0.32	0.14

Source: KOTIS, 2006. Author calculated depending on KOTIS database

This analysis is very helpful because the direct effect of trade liberalization under an FTA scheme will be on a bilateral trade pattern. Some analyses of factors influencing the success or failure of efforts to promote industrialization and growth conclude that a growing level of intra-industry trade (IIT) plays an important positive role. Intra-industry exchange produces extra gains from international trade over and above those associated with comparative advantage because it allows a country to take advantage of larger markets. By engaging in IIT, a country can simultaneously reduce the number of products while it increases the variety of available goods to domestic consumers.

Table Ⅲ-21 First Ten Biggest Commodities Shares of Trading Group 7(SITC 3-digit)

Commodity Code	Commodity(between China and Korea)
728	Other machinery, equipment specialized for industries
771	Electric power machinery and parts thereof
773	Equipment for distributing electricity, N.E.S
772	Electrical apparatus for switching
784	Parts of the motor vehicles
759	parts suitable for use with machines 751 and 752
752	Automatic data processing machines
778	Electrical machinery and apparatus N.E.S.
764	Telecommunications equipment, N.E.S
776	Valves, tubes

Source: KOTIS, 2006, Author calculated depending on KOTIS database

Table Ⅲ-22 First Ten Biggest Commodities of Group 7 between Korea and China in 2006

Code	Korea's Export to China	China's Export to Korea	share	IIT
728	1,436,652,223$	193,731,491$	3.13 %	0.24
771	700,366,708$	1,124,594,589$	3.51 %	0.77
773	933,808,120$	1,046,711,302$	3.80%	0.94
772	1,376,779,483$	1,314,471,559$	5.17 %	0.98
784	2,551,945,943$	285,887,829$	5.45 %	0.20

759	3,112,631,000$	1,914,772,489$	9.66%	0.76
752	2,997,233,695$	2,349,656,180$	10.27 %	0.88
778	2,589,540,809$	2,938,915,444$	10.62 %	0.94
764	5,676,709,117$	2,418,299,501$	15.55 %	0.60
776	6,580,514,542$	2,738,227,074$	17.90%	0.59

Source: KOTIS, 2006. Author calculated depending on KOTIS database

From the perspective of China's trade shares with Korea, machinery and transport equipment has become the biggest and most important groups both in Korea's export and import shares with China, and manufactured goods follow it ranking the second biggest trading group. So depending on the trade structures between Korea and China, the commodity group of machinery and transport equipment using SITC with 3-digit data has been chosen to analyze the specific trading features between Korea and China.

According to the SII analysis of group7 (SITC 3-digit) from table III-21 and III-22, the trading in group7 between Korea and China is showed to happen in an intra-industry pattern. And most of the ten biggest shares of trading commodities in group 7 have obvious intra-industry trade feature. Except for items 728 and 784, each commodity's average IIT-index is bigger than 0.8, which amounts to 76.5 percent of total trading commodity values in group 7. Therefore, most of the commodities in group 7 involved in trade between China and Korea have a feature of intra-industry trading, which reflects the general trade characteristics between the two countries.

Originating from this comprehensive analysis as to the trade between China and Korea, the following conclusions can be made. First, in the trade between the two partners, the trading share of manufactured products representing capital or labor-intensive sectors is much higher than that of resource-intensive agricultural products or primary products. The comparative advantages in different industries reflect the two countries' trading relations and trading competitiveness. RCA indices indicate China is more competitive in the commodity groups of 0, 2, 3, 4 such as food, crude materials, vegetables, and so on, which mostly mirror labor-intensive industries. Also, Koreans are strongly competitive in relative capital-intensive industries like chemicals, reflected by commodity group 5 (chemicals) and Korea's group 7 (machinery and transport equipment).

Second, the trade between Korea and China has strong complementarities and their intra-industry trade has been dominant. However, the trade competitiveness between them is gradually increasing with the expansion of bilateral trade volumes. And in intra-industry trade, the horizontal trading share is higher than vertical share in different segment of same industry. From the perspective of two countries' technology content, China's exporting products are endowed with relatively low added value. China disposes of strong trade competitiveness in low-tech products but it keeps decreasing and the comparative advantage is relatively stable. Owing to the improvement of the competition of foreign-invested companies, China's median and high-tech trading products has kept an upgrade trend but it mainly reflects China's foreign-invested companies' higher export structure levels and China's companies are still lacking in competitiveness compared to Korea. Therefore, Korea's technology content and added value of export products are generally higher than China's. In sum, if an FTA is concluded between Korea and China, intra-industry trade between the two countries will support a good basis for the trade deal itself and for intra-industry growth and overall economic gains in both countries.

CHAPTER

4

Theoretical Analysis
of the Korea-China FTA

01 | Analysis from FTA Theories

1.1. Trade Diversion and Trade Creation

Jakob Viner (1950) brought up the theory of trade diversion and trade creation from the formation of the preferential trade arrangement more than a half century ago. Trade diversion occurs when the participating countries in a regional grouping are not low-cost producers. In this sense the grouping may be an efficiency-reducing arrangement. Due to regional trade liberalization member countries acquire gain and advance over the extra-regional countries in terms of lower product prices granted by the reduction of tariffs and non-tariffs. A member country thus switches its imports from the more efficient rest of the world producers to the lesser efficient and higher cost partner country. This results in resource misallocation and amounts to trade diversion. Markets with trade diversion may generate national welfare losses. On the other hand, trade creation refers to the increase in trade among members of an RTA thanks to the elimination of tariffs on intra-regional trade. As Viner points out, imports would increase from within a trading bloc that the member country formerly did not import at all, and as a result, trade creation will likely generate far-reaching socio-economic profits.

The two concepts have become a core theory of regionalism and have induced intense discussions. It is common for economists to make the following statement: "If the positive effects from trade creation are larger than the negative effects from trade diversion, then the FTA will improve national welfare." A more succinct statement, though also somewhat less accurate, is that "if an FTA causes more trade creation than trade diversion then the FTA is improving welfare."[40] The empirical work on the subject, however, has proven to be challenging without explicit answers. Namely, whether trade creation is greater than trade diversion in an FTA is not an easy question to answer. According to Schiff and Winters, for FTAs involving developing countries, trade creation is substantial while trade diversion is either non-existent or small.[41] In a paper of Magee,[42] new estimates of trade creation and trade diversion are provided for each country signing a new FTA between 1985 and 1994. This research revealed that aggregate trade creation is approximately three times as large as trade diversion in the fifth year of these new trading blocs.

Another common thought on FTAs is the "natural trading partner hypothesis." This theory argues that regional trade agreements between nearby countries with significant bilateral trade are more likely to be trade-creating than trade-diverting. As a rule of thumb, an FTA should

---

40) Steven Suranovic,"Trade Diversion and Trade Creation" (1997-2004).

41) Schiff, Maurice and L. Alan Winters (2003).

42) Magee, 2004

be reasonably concluded on the same continent or among neighboring countries. This "good practice" best explains why most FTAs are sought after among regionally close neighbors. This hypothesis has been strongly supported by Wonnacott, Lutz, and Krugman.[43] But there are also differing points of view on the FTA / RTA question. Pravin Krishna[44] examines whether FTAs are natural in the sense that trade agreements with nearby countries and large trading partners are more beneficial. Empirical results don't support evidence toward the natural trading partner hypothesis. Magee[45] investigates the determinants of trade creation and trade diversion among country pairs that formed RTAs between 1985 and 1994. While nearby countries are more likely to sign preferential trade deals, according to Magee's findings, the agreements do not lead to more trade creation or less trade diversion. Probably the two scholars' arguments explain why FTAs in East Asia are seeking counterparts outside the region, even out of Asia. However, Magee's research manifests that country pairs with regional trade agreements consistently have higher levels of trade creation and lower levels of trade diversion than country pairs trading without preferences are predicted to have. Such results confirm the rationale for the proliferation of FTAs in the world.

According to international joint research on the effects of a CK-FTA, an FTAs such as the proposed CK-FTA contribute to worldwide trade liberalization by stimulating additional regional trade agreements and/or multilateral trade liberalization in order to minimize the damage of trade diversion. For instance, a CK-FTA would cause countries that export

---

43) Wonnacott and Lutz 1989; Krugman 1995.
44) Pravin Krishna, 2003.
45) Magee 2005.

agricultural goods to press Korea to lower tariffs on agricultural goods, which would ultimately benefit the Korean economy in general. This notion can be applied to the Chinese automobile industry. If a CK-FTA were to take effect, the EU and the United States may pressure China to reduce its tariffs. Therefore, a CK-FTA whose countries have core positions in many sectors, would tend to lead either to a broader FTA like an East Asia FTA, or to new FTAs with some countries outside of the region. Reduction in tariffs on multilateral levels would ultimately contribute to worldwide trade liberalization.

1.2. Domino Theory of FTAs

For a long time, the debate on trade creation versus trade diversion was confined to the static level ignoring dynamic time path issues. Put differently, expansion of FTA-memberships was simply treated as exogenous.[46] Only at the beginning of the 1990s, researchers began to think about regionalism as a dynamic process. Baldwin's domino theory is the first formal model to analyze the implications of trade diversion on membership in a particular RTA. Its basic assumption is that national trade policies are endogenous: they result from a political equilibrium balancing demand and supply of protection.

The conclusion of a new RTA implies a loss of competitiveness and lowers profits for non-member firms exporting to the regional bloc because they face entry barriers that members do not. As a consequence, these firms increase their pro-membership lobbying efforts, which will change the political equilibrium in their countries. The country whose government

---

46) Greenaway, 2000.

was closest to being indifferent to membership at the beginning will then join the RTA. This enlargement of the bloc increases the costs for non-members as the number of rivals with preferential market access has grown. As this cycle continues, additional countries will join like falling dominoes. The domino cycle only continues if the RTA in question is open and any country requesting membership is admitted.[47] In other words, the domino theory assumes that "the supply of membership is perfectly elastic."[48]

One domino effect began in the Western Hemisphere when the US and Mexico announced their intentions of forming a free trade area in 1990. Their motives were mainly geopolitical and philosophical. Announcement of the US-Mexico Free Trade Agreement (FTA) destroyed the political economy status quo in the Americas, thereby touching off a domino effect. Other North, Central and South American nations, which are heavily dependent on the US market, faced what appeared to be a fait accompli. Mexico-based producers would gain preferential access to the US market. This could be expected to harm the profits and market shares of firms based in third countries. Moreover, the preferential access to the US could be expected to divert foreign investment to Mexico at the expense of third countries. Canada, which depends very heavily on the US market, decided that it had to be at the negotiating table and the NAFTA was born. This choice was made despite continuing domestic opposition to its first regional liberalization - the US-Canada FTA. Other countries in the Hemisphere, such as Chile, Brazil, Argentina, Uruguay and Paraguay, formally or informally approached the US to begin bilateral FTA talks. Moreover, interest in President Bush's Enterprise

---

47) Roland Rieder, 2006.

48) Baldwin, 1993, p. 29.

for the Americas Initiative boomed in 1991 with 26 countries signing so-called Framework Agreements.[49]

Political economy forces driving the domino effect are strengthened by a peculiar tendency of special interest groups. They usually fight harder to avoid losses than they do to secure gains. In this light it is important that joining the regional integration in blocs would allow countries to avoid damage as well as to gain new commercial opportunities (Baldwin, 1993). From this theory, we can say that a CK-FTA can be considered a step to adapt to such a domino effect. Korea-China FTA is based on the 'domino theory of regionalism'. We start with a puzzle. Let us suppose that the level of a nation's import protection is determined by the balancing of pro-trade and anti-trade forces within each nation. The resulting protection is the level that the government finds optimal, after balancing all the demands it faces. If this is true, and it is, then trade liberalization is a bit of a puzzle. Why should a government find it politically optimal to remove barriers that previously it found optimal to maintain? The point of asking this question is to stress the necessity of focusing on what has change in the political arena. The domino theory is just one way of explaining how the signing of one FTA can change the arrangement of political forces in other nations.

A shock to a bilateral trade relationship – the Korea-China FTA in this case – can trigger requests for further FTAs from countries whose governments(Such as Japan) were previously happy without FTAs. The basic logic is simple. The stance of a country's government concerning an FTA is the result of a political equilibrium that balances anti-FTA

---

49) RICHARD E. BALDWIN

and pro-FTA forces. Since closer integration between Korea and China is detrimental to the profits of firms based in other nations - this being due mainly to the preferences that the FTA grants Korean firms in the Chinese market – the FTA signing stimulates exporters in other Asian nations to engage in greater pro-FTA political activity. Now if one of the other nations' governments was previously close to indifferent, politically speaking, to signing an FTA with China then the extra political activity of their exporters may tilt the balance, leading the country to sign an FTA. This can be thought of as one domino knocking down the next one (think of the first FTA signing as someone pushing over the first domino, and the second FTA as the second domino falling). To be a bit more explicit, if Korea signs an FTA with Japan, then other Asian nations are also likely to want an FTA with Korea. After all, the Korea-China FTA gives Korean firms an advantage in the big Chinese market and this, quite directly, puts non-Korean firms at a disadvantage in the Chinese market. The only way to counter this new disadvantage is to push for an FTA with China. The story does not stop here, however. After the second FTA is signed, firms based in two Asian nations have preferential access to China. And this, in turn, puts firms based in non-FTA nations at an even greater disadvantage than when faced with only the Korea-China FTA, since a wider range of their competitors enjoys preferential access. As a result, non-FTA firms will have to cut their prices and accept smaller shares of the Chinese market as a result of the second FTA. In the political sphere this new disadvantage will result in greater political pressure - pressure on their own governments to negotiate an FTA with China - from the exporters who have lost. If the government of a third nation was previously close to indifferent to signing, this extra pressure may tilt the balance in favor of an FTA. A third FTA gets signed with China. And the cycle repeats.

The basic idea is that costs of not having an FTA with China rise as more of your competitors have them. Thus the political pressure that non-FTA governments face from their exporter is likely to rise as more and more FTAs are signed. This process only stops if everyone who really depends upon the Chinese market is in, or if the non-FTA governments have very strong non-economic reasons for staying away from FTAs. Notice that this Asian-dominos story is much closer to the North American story. Preferential trade agreements in America are bilateral — even NAFTA is just a collection of 3 bilateral FTAs (US-Canada, US-Mexico and Mexico-Canada). As a consequence, the automatic market-size effect does not kick in the North American case. Nor will it in the Asian case — at least if things evolve they will, namely in a hub-and-spoke manner.

1.3. Rules of Origins (ROOs) and the Spaghetti Bowl Theory

Rules of Origin refer to the criteria used to define where a product was made under the definition of World Trade Organization (WTO). In general, ROOs exist as an essential part of trade agreements since there is a need to distinguish between different foreign sources of a given product.[50] The importance of ROOs has grown significantly as preferential agreements expand and countries have treated similar imported goods differently according to where the product was made.

---

50) Coyle, 2004.

The "spaghetti bowl phenomenon" is often cited as a problem of free trade agreements. The proliferation of regional trade agreements has necessarily been accompanied by the proliferation of ROOs[51] due to its discriminative tariffs and non-tariff differences between the members and non-members of FTAs. The labyrinthine rules of origin have undeniably made international trade more costly and complex.[52] The presence of complex rules of origin would make it difficult to determine the country of origin, resulting in higher business and administration costs. When different complex rules of origin apply to different FTAs, things are even more complicated: both companies and governments would find them more difficult to understand and more costly to use. Such is how some people understand the spaghetti bowl phenomenon. The term was first used by Jagdish Bhagwati.[53] Subsequently, he has used the term on various occasions in describing a problem of FTAs. Also, due to its charm, the use of term spread quickly. The spaghetti bowl phenomenon as referred to by Bhagwati is an inevitable result of FTAs that reduce or eliminate tariffs on imports from specific countries and cannot be circumvented simply by changing the shaping of FTAs.

Bhagwati found it problematic that an FTA creates an artifact production network of countries that would not be consistent with the principle of economic efficiency. By this, he was referring to the manner in which half-finished products and parts go around various FTA networks using tariff differentiation in an effort to export finished products to the consumer countries at the lowest price. He visualized this as crisscrossing lines and

---

51) Harilal and Beena, 2003.

52) WTO, 2003.

53) Jagdish Bhagwati, 1995.

likened these strings of lines to strands of spaghetti tangled in a bowl. By building trade liberalization on the foundation of discrimination, FTAs create a fundamental conflict with multilateralism. This proliferation of the ROO from FTAs has led to a crisscrossing of trade preferences assigned to countries. Hence, the products depending on where they supposedly originate from different markets have to suffer from the complicated "spaghetti bowl", which will increase trade costs for FTA members. Actually, the ability to identify the country of origin for products is increasingly problematic owing to the globalization of production.

■ Rules of Origin in China's FTAs

China applies non-preferential rules of origin in accordance with the Regulations on Rules of Origin of Import and Export Commodities. For goods wholly obtained within one country or region, that country or region shall be regarded as the origin of the goods. For goods of which the production involves two or more countries or regions, the country or region where the last substantial transformation has been made shall be regarded as the origin of the product. Substantial transformation shall be determined based on the changes in tariff classification criterion. In cases where the changes of tariff classification cannot reflect the substantial transformation, the percentage of ad valorem, working procedures of manufacturing or processing, etc. shall be used as supplementary criteria. The Regulations on Rules of Origin of Import and Export Commodities also provides for the legal framework of China on ad-ministration of Rules of Origin matters. Preferential rules of origin of China are applicable to products originating from countries or regions with which China has concluded preferential trade arrangements (PTAs), such as Free Trade Agreements (FTAs) and Regional Trade Arrangements (RTAs). The primary criteria of Preferential Rules of Origin are the wholly obtained and substantial transformation criteria. Substantial transformation criteria include change in tariff classification criterion, regional value content criterion, manufacturing process criterion, or combination of the criteria mentioned above. China's FTAs with ASEAN, Chile, Pakistan, Singapore, and RTAs/PTAs with APTA participant countries and preferential measures (Zero-tariff treatment) for least developed countries mainly use the regional value content criterion, while China's FTAs with New Zealand, Peru and Costa Rica mainly use the change in tariff classification criterion, supplemented by the regional value content and the manufacturing process criteria. Regarding the substantial transformation criteria adopted under various China's FTAs, a product-specific rules of origin list had been set out for products to be granted originating status. Be- sides, the imported goods must meet the direct transport rule to apply for preferential rules of origin. Preferential rules of origin also cover related operational procedures, including issuance of certificates of origin, checking of certificate of origin and the goods at the time of importation and exportation, as the case may be, and verification based on negotiated procedures between the Parties. In most FTAs signed by China, a Certificate of Origin serves as the certificating document of the origin of the imported goods.

APTA

Products must be wholly obtained or produced in the member country, or the value of non-originating parts or components used in the manufacture must be no more than 55% of the FOB value of the product. The country of origin is defined as the country where the last processing operation takes place. In addition, goods must meet the direct transport rule.

China-ASEAN

Products must be wholly obtained or produced in ASEAN countries; or the content of products originating in any one of the ASEAN countries should be no less than 40% of total content; or the value of the non-originating parts or components used in the manufacture of the products must be no more than 60% of the f.o.b. value of the product. The country of origin is de- fined as the country where the last processing operation takes place. In addition, goods must meet the direct transport rule.

CEPA Hong Kong

Products must be wholly produced in Hong Kong, China or have Hong Kong, China content of at least 30% of value added; in addition, the final stage of processing must be carried out in Hong Kong, China. Goods must enter into Mainland China directly.

CEPA Macao

China Products must be wholly produced in Macao, China or have Macao, China content of at least 30% of value added or have resulted in a change in the HS 4-digit tar-iff heading; in addition, the final stage of processing must be carried out in Macao, China. In addition, goods must meet the direct transport rule.

China-Chile FTA

Products must be wholly obtained or produced in Chile, or the value of non-originating parts or components used in the manufacture must be less than 60% of the f.o.b. value of the product. The country of origin is de-fined as the country where the last processing operation takes place. In addition, goods must meet the direct transport rule.

China-Pakistan FTA

Products must be wholly obtained or produced in Pakistan, or the value of non-originating parts or components used in the manufacture must be less than 60% of the FOB value of the product. The country of origin is defined as the country where the last processing operation takes place. In addition, goods must meet the direct transport rule.

China-New Zealand FTA

Products must be wholly obtained or produced in New Zealand, or products be produced in New Zealand, using non-originating materials that conform to a change in tariff classification (some products must also be con- form to a regional value content or a process requirement). In addition, goods must meet the direct transport rule.

China-Singapore FTA

Products must be wholly obtained or produced in Singapore; or the percentage of regional value content shall not be less than 40% of the product. In addition, goods must meet the direct transport rule.

China-Peru FTA

Products must be wholly obtained or produced in Peru, or products be produced in Peru, using non-originating materials that conform to a change in tariff classification (some products must also be conform to a regional value content or a process requirement). In addition, goods must meet the direct transport rule.

■ Rules of Origin in Korea's FTAs

Korea has maintained the principle that an originating status can be conferred upon an imported good when it is "wholly obtained or produced" or undergoes "substantial transformation process" in the Parties to the FTA. In order to determine whether a good undergoes a substantial transformation process, the change of tariff classification (CTC) is generally used and is supplemented by value-added and a specific process criterion. The CTC has also been a most preferred standard in the on-going negotiations on the WTO Harmonized Rules of Origin as well as in other FTAs. Korea's FTA also contains other rules considered in conferring the origin status, such as accumulation, intermediate materials, neutral elements, direct consignment and non-qualifying operations. As regards the Kaesong Industrial Complex Project (KICP), all the FTAs that Korea has concluded reflect in their respective texts appropriate language referring to the KICP.

Korea-Singapore FTA

1. The goods listed in Annex 4B shall be originating goods, when the goods are imported into the territory of Singapore from the territoriality of Korea. The goods shall also be originating materials for purposes of satisfying the requirements specified in this Chapter.
2. Upon request of a Party, the Parties shall have consultations on the operation or revision of this Article and Annex 4B.

Korea-EFTA FTA

Notwithstanding the provisions of Article 12, the acquisition of originating status in accordance with the conditions set out in Title II shall not be affected by working or processing carried out outside the territoriality of a Party on materials exported from the Party concerned and subsequently re-imported there, provided that the conditions set out in Appendix 4 are fulfilled.

Korea-ASEAN FTA

Notwithstanding Rules 2, 4 and 5, certain goods shall be considered to be originating even if the production process or operation has been undertaken in an area outside the territories of Korea and ASEAN Member Countries (i.e. industrial zone) on materials exported from a Party and subsequently re-imported to that Party. The application of this Rule, including the list of products and the specific procedures related to this application shall be mutually agreed upon by the Parties.

Korea-US FTA

Recognizing the Republic of Korea's constitutional mandate and security interests, and the corresponding interests of the United States, the Parties shall establish a Committee on Outward Processing Zones on the Korean Peninsula. The Committee shall review whether conditions on the Korean Peninsula are appropriate for further economic development through the establishment and development of outward processing zones.

■ Suggestions for Korea-China FTA ROO

A CKFTA may follow the several principles mentioned below:
¾ Preferential ROO are established to identify whether goods qualify for preferential tariff treatment under a CKFTA.
¾ ROO should serve to promote bilateral trade and investment.

¾ ROO should be simple, transparent, predictable and user-friendly.

¾ Trade circumvention from third countries should be minimized.

As a principle, only originating goods in China and Korea should benefit from tariff elimination under a CKFTA. In addition, throughout the discussions within the framework of the Joint Study, Korea has taken the view that given the importance and possible role of the Kaesong Industrial Complex Project, a possible CKFTA should include in its ROO section appropriate provisions allowing goods produced in Kaesong and other outward processing zones on the Korean peninsula to enjoy originating status.[54]

1.4. Hub and Spoke Theory

The recent proliferation of bilateral agreements has created a number of "hub-and-spokes" types of trade relationship, i.e., one economy becomes a "hub" by establishing bilateral agreements with a number of other nations (the "spokes"). This has been especially noticeable in the East Asia Region. China, Japan, South Korea and ASEAN, in particular, have adopted very ambitious and aggressive bilateral liberalization agendas, at present forming as many FTAs as possible. An interesting stylized fact of global trade is the proliferation of regional trade agreements (RTAs), including overlapping free trade agreements (FTAs). Many of the FTAs are overlapping and allow some countries to become a hub in the production networks of FTAs. On the one hand, relative to non-hub countries, an FTA-hub country gains preferential access to more markets and thus enjoys improved export competitiveness. To the extent that

---

54) The Joint Study Report for China-Korea FTA

such an advantage translates into more exports, the hub-and-spoke feature of overlapping FTAs can have a positive effect on trade.

The Hub-and-Spoke of configuration has numerous economic implications, many of which are similar to those found in the standard literature on preferential or discriminatory trade policy. From the viewpoint of the hub, the system is beneficial since it provides preferential access to the market of each spoke. The hub also provides free access to each spoke so that effectively it can move closer to a unilateral free trade regime, which means that the potential adverse terms-of-trade impact of trade diversion is limited. At the same time, the degree of competition will be more intense in the hub's market, which may hurt domestic firms but benefit consumers. While each spoke has free trade with the hub, the discriminatory nature of the FTA moves it away from free trade with other spokes. Spoke-to-spoke trade would suffer as trade is diverted toward the hub: it is relatively more advantageous to import from the hub, as it is to export to the hub's market. Each spoke loses from being discriminated against in all the different FTAs from which it is excluded. Even the market access gains from the FTA with the hub would be diluted since the hub is giving the same (if not more favorable) preference to all the other spokes.[55]

Innwon Park analyzed the effects of possible Hub-and-Spoke patterns of FTA in East Asia with CGE models. He found additional positive trade creation effects to original members (hub) as the existing RTAs expand. Such "expansions" unevenly distribute more welfare and output gains for a hub compared to relatively smaller gains for spokes. This disparity explains why FTAs driven by the hub-and spoke pattern are

---

55) Gouranga Gopal Das and Soamiely Andriamananjara, 2006.

proliferating in East Asia. Therefore, we can conclude from the hub-and-spoke theory that both Korea and China desire to create as many FTAs as possible to become the hub of the FTA network. A considerable number of studies have proved the rationale for such a motive.

On the other hand, as Lloyd and MacLaren (2004) point out, in an FTA-hub country, exporters and importers face multiple sets of rules of origin (ROOs), which can lead to costs related to the verification of such rules. These additional costs can, in turn, restrain trade creation. Therefore, being an FTA hub within the network of FTAs does not necessarily have a positive effect on exports. The hub-and-spoke nature of FTAs has been analyzed at length in the trade literature. Early country--specific studies on hub-and-spoke systems include analysis of Canadian FTA policy by Wonnacott (1975, 1982). In addition, Kowalczyk and Wonnacott (1992) investigated hub-and-spoke systems within the context of the North American Free Trade Agreement (NAFTA). More recent studies include, among others, Benedictis et al. (2005) on the European Union (EU)-15 and Central and Eastern Europe; Deltas et al. (2006) on Israel; and Chong and Hur (2008) on Singapore, Japan, and the United States (US). For our purposes, the most relevant study is Lee et al. (2008), which empirically examined the trade effects of what they refer to as —overlapping RTAs‖ using the dataset from Rose (2004). They built a panel dataset comprising 175 countries from 1948 to 1999 and used an augmented gravity model with dummies representing several features of overlapping RTAs. They estimated the trade diversion and creation effects of overlapping RTAs and showed that overlapping RTAs are ultimately undesirable for global trade due to the dominance of the trade diversion effect. [56]

An analysis of the welfare effects of three different types of FTA formation between technically asymmetric countries has been based on a simple oligopoly model: representative firms with asymmetric technology from each country compete in the so-called "Cournot fashion" providing for the following results. When Korea takes the sequential FTA strategy, i.e., first creating the Korea-Japan FTA followed by the Korea-ASEAN FTA, and in the CK-FTA with significant time gaps, the producer surplus of the country with intermediate technology levels, such as Korea, turn out to be deteriorated. This is a Hub-and-Spoke type FTA strategy, where Korea forms multiple bilateral FTAs such as the one between Korea and Japan. In a Korea-ASEAN FTA and a China-Korea FTA simultaneously, the Korean social welfare and producer surpluses turn out to be increased significantly. The welfare effect of a multilateral FTA arrangement, that is to form a China-Korea-Japan FTA from the initial stage, turns out to be lower than that of the Hub-and-Spoke type FTA, however, still higher than that from the Sequential FTA strategy. The simulation results with the actual data on the technology gap show that Korean producer surplus decreases by 20.16% from the sequential FTA strategy while it increases 11.48% from the Hub-and-Spoke type FTA strategy. Therefore, from this theory, we also conclude the China-Korea FTA would turn out to be a big step forward for the two countries to push themselves to the FTA hub as they are presently strong trade partners with each other.

What 'hub-and-spoke' goes to say is that if Asian regionalism gets rolling, it is likely that a string of FTAs will be signed between China/Korea/Japan/ASEAN with other nations. In other words, it would result in a 'hub-and-spoke' trade arrangement with one nation

---

56) Joseph Alba, Jung Hur, and Donghyun Park (2010)

as the hub and the other partners as the spokes due to the competition process and presently ASEAN has achieve such a goal with the formation of three "10+1"FTA. The point is that many Asian nations rely fairly heavily on the Chinese market, but other trade flows in Asia are more modest, which is being driving China-Korea FTA going much fast.

02 | Need for a Korea-China FTA: Alternative Thinking

2.1. Promotion of Bilateral Intra-Industry Trade and Comparative Advantages

China is an enormous market with 9.60 million square kilometers of territory and 1.3 billion people, whereas Korea has less than 100 thousand square kilometers of territory and more than 45 million people, with a limited market and resource capacity. Regarding factor endowments, the per capita land in Korea (0.30 hectares) is only half of that in China (0.76 hectares) but the per capita capital of Korea ($2427.5) is nearly 10 times the figure for the individual Chinese ($282.7). Such a fundamental status difference indicates that China has obvious advantages in developing agriculture while Korea has an advantage in developing manufacturing.[57]

To fully understand the competitive and complementary relations in industries between China and Korea, I have performed a qualitative analysis by using the regional RCA and IIT methods. My calculation

---

57) Zhang Jianping (2006).

results indicate that many industries between the two countries are strongly complementary. China's comparative advantage over Korea is mainly in primary and labor-intensive sectors, such as food, crude materials, and vegetables. Korea's competitive comparative advantage over China is mainly in capital-intensive sectors, especially in chemicals, machinery and transport equipment. Competition between the two countries is focused on manufacturing products. There are a great number of intra-industry trades as analyzed in chapter 3. There are several features of industry division of China and Korea. The first is the obvious overall complementariness between both countries, with complementary industries occupying more than half of the total. The complementary scope is further expanded by some industries with intra-industry trade. This is the result of the clear difference in the factor endowments between them. The second is processing trade, which dominates intra-industry trade from both sides. The third is the increasingly narrowing gap, diminishing complementariness, and intensifying competition in manufacturing between China and Korea. The fourth are the ever-complicating forms of intra-industry trade between China and Korea. Vertical division and horizontal division go hand in hand, in addition to which there is a large amount of intra-industry trade. Overall, the industries of both countries are more complementary than competitive.

2.2. A Buffer for the Economic and Political Tensions

It is often pointed out that some non-economic factors, such as the rivalry of maritime rights between China and South Korea, differences in political systems, territory problem such as Gaogouli area, and some disputes of traditional festivals (Duan wu festival issue) presently count among the important obstacles to deepen economic integration. The importance of these non-economic factors can't be overlooked in route to the economic cooperation between the two countries.

A 1990s World Bank report pointed out that diverse political factors were the main motives behind the expansion of trade blocs in the 1990s.[58] The early history of regional trade pact shows a well-known case of strategic regionalism. The main objective of European economic integration was to prevent a new war in Europe, and economic cooperation was the means to achieving this goal.[59] However, if we look at these issues from another perspective, those non-economical factors deemed as obstacles could actually be objectives of the KC FTA. An FTA would help to promote a community consciousness and harmonize the political systems between China and Korea.

Another key point is the nuclear weapon issue caused by North Korea. As a well-known fact, North Korea frequently conducts nuclear tests for many reasons. A CK-FTA could stimulate North Korean reform, providing additional benefits to the countries in the region. Peace in the peninsula can be maintained under the cooperation between Korea, China, America, Russia, Japan and other countries. Once a FTA has been activated, an organized process between China and Korea would usher in peace and development to the Northeast Asian region. To a large degree, a CK-FTA would ultimately contribute significantly to peace and prosperity of Northeast Asia by easing military tension.

---

58) World Bank, 2000.

59) Schiff, M. and L. A. Winters, As early as 1775, Immanuel Kant argued that increases in economic exchanges between countries could deter war (Schiff and Winters, p. 271), May 1988.

2.3. Restructuring two Countries' Vulnerable Domestic Industries

A KC FTA can serve as a channel through which to advance the competitiveness of the two countries by promoting a restructuring of vulnerable domestic industries within them. As mentioned earlier, even though a CK-FTA would bring positive macroeconomic effects by increasing the GDP and the welfare of the people, the two countries have vulnerable industries which would incur losses from an FTA. For instance, Korea's agriculture suffers from a relatively low competitiveness. The government has fixed very high tariffs to protect domestic agriculture from overseas competition. Those who are engaged in such vulnerable industries would oppose a CK-FTA, and politicians may surrender to pressure from interest groups to avoid social and political costs. However, prolonged protection of vulnerable industries will decrease the competitiveness of the whole economy. A country may incur enormous economic costs through the distortion of resource allocation. Moreover, it can lead to a vicious circle of low growth and high unemployment. Therefore, each country must propel the restructuring of vulnerable industries.

A CK-FTA will contribute to advancing the competitiveness of the two countries by promoting the restructuring of vulnerable industries. In fact, some countries join FTAs to guarantee economic reform. For instance, one of the main reasons Mexico joined NAFTA was to prevent the possibility of a reversal in domestic economic reform by the next administration.[60] Domestic political pressure from interest groups related to each country's vulnerable industries can be overcome only when a

---

60) Whalley, John, 1998.

package plan of education, vocational training, and compensation is in place, combined with a firm plan for restructuring.

Within the context of a possible FTA between China and Korea, both sides would need to more concretely discuss ways of enhancing their cooperation in such areas as Transparency, SMEs, Technology Cooperation (E-commerce, S&T, IT), Energy Cooperation and Environmental Cooperation. To this end, it would be desirable to seek to streamline and strengthen the existing cooperative mechanisms, such as the high-level channel for dialogue on the environment. The 2005 "Joint Study on the China-Korea Economic and Trade Cooperation Vision," which was announced in Nov. 2005 on the occasion of the China-Korea Summit in Seoul, would also serve as a good reference as both sides work together to bring their bilateral economic partnership to new heights.

2.4. A Proof from Regionalism

Moreover, as for adjoining countries in the same region, geographic advantages will help to support regional integrity to guarantee more facilitated economic cooperation. From the point of economic theory, there are many cultural advantages belonging to the organization formed by adjoining countries, such as the facilitation in exchange of labors and commodities and similarities in language and culture. Adjoining and non-adjoining countries and regions both can benefit from enlarging and enhancing the economic cooperation, but because of the "strong complementarities" caused by geographic advantage and differences between population, economic development some countries signed bilateral FTAs. Such a theory has proved its rationale and feasibility. Thus, a CK-FTA will make full use of geographic and cultural advantages to aid bilateral benefits.

In November 2004, during the APEC Summit Meeting in Chile, President Hu Jintao of the People's Republic of China, and President Roh Moo-Hyun of the Republic of Korea, agreed to a non-governmental feasibility study on a China- Korea FTA (CKFTA), and expressed their desire to obtain the results yielded by the joint research at an early time.The Development Research Center of the State Council of China and the Korea Institute for International Economic Policy conducted a two-year joint "Feasibility Study for the China-Korea FTA" from 2005 to 2006. Completed in 2006, this research drew a conclusion that the FTA would be mutually beneficial and win-win for both countries. In November 2006, China and ROK decided to upgrade the unofficial study to a study to be jointly made by government, business and academia. Major work has been done thanks to the joint efforts by the two sides. Currently, the two sides are hard working on a few remaining issues unable to be agreed on. In 2010, Chinese Premier Wen Jiabao and President of South Korea Lee Myung-bak held a talk. Both parties announced to wrap up China and ROK government-industry-university joint study in Free Trade Area (FTA) with the MOU signed by bilateral economic and trade ministers. The joint study has deepened mutual understanding and taken an important step in the process of the FTA between the countries to lay a good foundation for further promoting the construction of China-ROK FTA. Both parties agreed to further exchange opinions on their own concerns next to create conditions for launching talks in future.

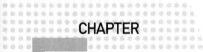

CHAPTER

5

Potential Economic Effects
of a Korea-China FTA

01 | CGE Models and Global Trade Analysis Project System

1.1. Introduction of the CGE model

General-equilibrium analysis involves using a specified general- equilibrium model for policy evaluation. Over the last several decades, Computable General Equilibrium (CGE) models have become an important tool for analyzing economic issues. This development is explained by the strong capability of CGE models to explain the economic impacts and behaviors including the linkages between all agents, sectors and economies. The CGE model embraces domestic factors of production, consumption, investment, governmental expenditure and the external factors such as export and import. It computes the optimal solutions of the impact of domestic and overseas policy changes. The CGE model is a system of simultaneous equations which are used to describe economic agents' behaviors, such as production, consumption, trade, and investment.

When some change occurs in one variable due to some real-world changes, it alters the size of other related variables. Every variable is interconnected and therefore the accounting system is difficult to calculate by hand, so the computation process has to be implemented by computers. The CGE model enables us to quantitatively derive changes in national production and welfare together with trade and caused by a certain shock which allows both domestic and international inter-industrial interactions. The CGE model is widely used not only to analyze the effects of changes in trade policy such as a regional trade agreement and multilateral trade liberalization negotiations for each country and industry. But it also explains the effect of policies such as international environmental agreements and bilateral investment agreements on the domestic and international economy.

In order to get some insight into the implications and analyze the potential impact of a Korea-China FTA, some simulations are made with CGE model. General equilibrium refers to the study of models in which equilibrium is simultaneously obtained in all markets. CGE models try to turn the abstract general equilibrium theory into a practical tool which can be used for policy analysis. In the basic CGE model, optimizing behavior is explicitly built through the utility maximization conditions, which forms the basis of expenditure function and the profit maximization conditions underlying the cost functions. Meanwhile, economy-wide constraints are enforced, as the conditions underlying the expenditure functions reflect. And CGE models capture the relationships between demand and supply in each market. Typical CGE model adds more modifications such as the introduction of intermediate inputs in production and final demands distinguished between households, government, producer, trade, and capital creation. Multi-regional CGE models also incorporate imperfect substitution between foreign and domestic goods and between alternative sources of imports, which is known as the Armington Assumption.[61] Because CGE models are usually designed for policy analysis, most models will also incorporate a variety of distortions, most commonly in the form of taxes, tariff or subsidy on various economic activities in different markets. The key point of CGE model is that choosing different closures means having a significant impact on the model results. And various specifications have been used to introduce imperfect competition into CGE models, which may cause an important impact on model results.

In general, the starting point of CGE model will be a national input-output table or data, and a set of trade matrices in multiregional models. These data represent the state of the economy in the base year. Also, specific functional forms must be employed to define the substitution relationships of a CGE model. Once the functional forms are decided, free parameters are obtained by either econometric estimation or literature searches. Profit and utility maximizing conditions are then assumed to hold in the base year, allowing the remaining parameters to be determined from the base data, a process called calibration. Simulation in most CGE models involves examining comparative static results. CGE models have no explicit time dimension, and instead represent different time frames by altering microeconomic elements of the closure. The results of static simulations are often as representation on how the economic system in question would have looked, if the new policy had been in place in the base year, after all relevant adjustments have taken place.[62]

Having introduced the basic CGE models and provided an overview of the way in which CGE model is constructed and used, a brief overview

---

61) Armington, "a theory of demand for products distinguished by place of production," *IMF Staff Papers (16)*, 1969, pp. 159-178.

62) JOHN P. GILBERT, "Appendix B GTAP Model Analysis: Simulating the Effect of a Korea-US FTA Using Computable General Equilibrium Techniques", 2001.

will be given on how the model will be used in this study. Shoven and Whalley once stated, despite the widespread use of the term "general equilibrium" in modern economics, the precise meaning of the term is often not fully defined. Everyone seems to agree that a general-equilibrium model is one in which all markets clear in equilibrium; there seems to be less agreement as to the essential elements of structure which underlie the equilibrium formulation.[63] The standardized CGE model has the advantage of reducing expenses and deducing verified results, as a policy experiment costs a great deal of time and data. This study utilizes a standard GTAP model and GEMPACK software, and a GTAP database.

1.2. The Global Trade Analysis Project (GTAP) and Its Model Structures

The Global Trade Analysis Project (GTAP) is a research program initiated in 1992 to provide the economic research community with a global economic dataset for use in the quantitative analyses of international economic issues. The Project's objectives include the provision of a documented, publicly available, global general equilibrium data base, and to inform the research community about how to use the data in applied economic analysis. GTAP has lead to the establishment of a global network of researchers who share a common interest of multi-region trade analysis and related issues.[64]

---

63) John B. Shoven; John Whalley, "Applied General-Equilibrium Models of Taxation and International Trade: An Introduction and Survey", *Journal of Economic Literature*, Vol. 22, No. 3, (Sep, 1984), pp.1008-1009.

64) Thomas F. Rutherford, "GTAP in GAMS: The Dataset and Static Model", University of Colorado, 1998.

Table V-1 Different Data and Elasticities in GTAP Model

No	Classifications
1	The data of bilateral trade flows
2	Protection data for merchandise trade such as tariffs and subsidies
3	Input and output (I-O) tables of different countries
4	Factor substitution elasticities
5	Source substitution elasticities (Armington)
6	Behavioral parameters for households
7	Factor transformation elasticities……

Source: From GTAP Version 6.0

The Project consists of several components: (1). Global data base and a standard general equilibrium modeling framework, (2). Software which is used to deal with the data base and standard models. (3). A global network of over 1200 researchers and a consortium of agencies. GTAP is usually used to analyze issues that cut across many diverse sectors. This data base is particularly popular with researchers analyzing the potential impact such as global trade liberalization under a future WTO round, the effects of regional trade agreements, and domestic impacts of economic shocks in other regions. Sector-by-sector analyses of these questions can provide a valuable input into studies of these issues. However, by their very nature, these shocks affect all sectors and many regions of the world, so there is no way to avoid employing a data base which is exhaustive in its coverage of commodities and countries. The Global Trade Analysis Project is just designed to facilitate such multi-country, economy-wide analyses.[65]

The key ingredient of GTAP's success has been in its global data

---

65) Hertel, T.W., ed, "Global Trade Analysis: Modeling and Applications." New York, Cambridge University Press, 1997.

base which combines detailed bilateral trade, transport and protection data characterizing economic linkages among regions, together with individual country input-output data bases which account for intersectional linkages within regions. The data used for this research come from published sources from GTAP 6.0. The database provides disaggregated data of 87 regions across a maximum of 57 sectors. All monetary values of the data are expressed in US dollar (millions) and the reference year is 2001

The GTAP model is based on assumptions such as constant returns to scale, perfect competition and a global bank designed to mediate between world savings and investment. The Constant Difference of Elasticity (CDE) consumer demand system is designed to capture differential prices and income responsiveness across countries. The GTAP modeling framework consists of a static computable general equilibrium model and a global database on international trade. The underlying equation system of GTAP includes two different kinds of equations. One covers the accounting relationships which can ensure that receipts and expenditures of each agent are balanced. The other equation system consists of behavioral equations which base on microeconomic theory. These equations specify the behavior of optimizing agents in the economy, such as demand functions.[66]

There are two imagined international sectors defined as Global bank and Global transportation. A "global bank" ensures that the global demand for savings equals the global demand for investment in the post-solution equilibrium. The global bank assembles savings and disburses investment through the sales of a homogenous savings commodity to regional households in order for them to purchase a composite investment good and hold

---

66) Martina BROCKMEIER, "A Graphical Exposition of the GTAP Model", *GTAP Technical Paper No. 8*, 2001.

shares in a portfolio of net regional investments (Considering Gross Investment= Net Investment + Depreciation, here gross investment less depreciation). Savings and investment do not have to be equal at the regional level. A region saves by buying the savings commodity. At the same time, it produces capital goods. These goods are sold by the global bank together with other regions' capital goods as a portfolio in the form of a composite investment good. Savers claim shares in this portfolio depending on how much of the savings commodity they buy. In addition to the global bank, there is another global agent called global transportation sector which is required in this model in order to intermediate between the supply of international transport services and demand for it. These services are provided via Cobb-Douglas production function. Lacking the data to link exports of transport services with specific routes, GTAP simply combines all these services into a single composite international transport good, which is used to balance the value between the CIF price and FOB price.

In a Multi-Region Open Economy (See figureV-1), the GTAP models include all single countries and regions which connect with each other by trade flows. The GTAP model employs the Armington assumption in the trading sector which can distinguish imports by origin. Thus, imported commodities are assumed to be separable from domestically produced goods and combined in an additional nested part in the production tree. The elasticity of substitution in this input nest is equal across all uses. Under these circumstances, the firms decide first on the sourcing of their imports and based on the resulting composite import price, and then they then determine the optimal mix of imported and domestic goods.[67] Considering GTAP database 6.0 version covers 87 regions,

---

67) Ibidem, p15

one region is chosen to show the changes in the model structure and all the other regions are combined into a sector named Rest of the World (RoW), which is quite necessary for us to model an open economy. Because these changes happen in every region of the multi region model, a complete overview could be shown by this approach.

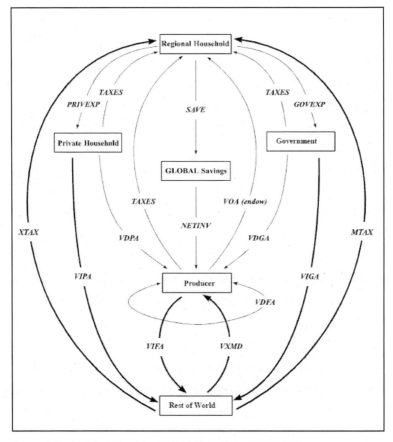

Source: A Graphical Exposition of the GTAP Model by Martina BROCKMEIER

Figure V-1 Multi Region Open Economy

Figure V-1 represents a multi-region open economy in which the accounting relationships of all agents are shown. "Regional household" is assumed as a representative regional decision-maker lying at the top level of the demand function tree. In the production side, the producers receive revenues for selling consumption goods to the private households *(VDPA)* and the government *(VDGA)*, intermediate inputs to other producers *(VDFA)* and investment goods to the savings sector *(NETINV)*. At the same time, the firms also get additional revenues for selling commodities to the RoW. These exports are denoted by *VXMD*. Under the zero profit assumption employed in GTAP, these revenues must be precisely exhausted on expenditures for intermediate inputs *(VDFA)* and primary factors of production *(VOA)*. Here, the producers spend their revenues not only on primary factors and domestically produced intermediate inputs, but also on imported intermediate inputs, *VIFA*.[68]

TAXES flows in the GTAP model also can be demonstrated in figure V-1. First of All, *TAXES* flow from the private household, firms and the government to the regional household. At the same time, additional *TAXES* also flow from the RoW to the regional household. Since these value flows denote net tax revenues, including both taxes and subsidies. The private households spend their incomes not only on domestically produced commodities, but also on imported commodities which are denoted as *VIPA*, and so does the government (denoted as *VIGA)*. Furthermore, both agents have to pay additional commodity taxes on imports to the regional household, so that the accounting relationships of these two agents now also include consumption taxes and expenditure for imported commodities. Producers are also the object of taxation.

---

68) Ibidem, p14

Firms also have to pay *TAXES* to the regional household. Furthermore, the firms have to pay an additional consumption tax on imported inputs to the regional household. Since this tax expenditure is included in the *TAXES* flowing from the producers to the regional household. All *TAXES* levied in the economy always accrue to the regional household. As a result, the regional income consists of *VOA* paid for the use of *endowment commodities* and the sum over all taxes minus subsidies.

A. Producer's Behavior in Production Side

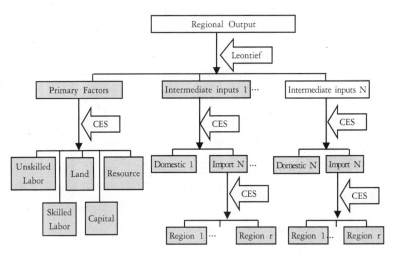

Figure V-2 Production Structures of the GTAP Model

On the production side (see figure V-2), firms use intermediate inputs and primary factors of production. The derived demands for inputs are based on the profit-maximizing behavior of firms. All markets are assumed perfectly competitive so that firms earn zero profits at the equilibrium status.

Production in every sector exhibits constant returns to scale and can be divided into two levels. First, domestic and imported intermediates are used to produce a composite intermediate. Demanders treat imports from different sources as imperfect substitutes. Primary factors are used to produce a new item called value-added. This level is characterized by no substitution possibilities between the intermediate inputs and the primary factors of production. However, substitution is possible among the primary factors and among the intermediates. The demands in each case are represented by a constant elasticity substitution (CES) function. At the final stage, both the value-added and the composite intermediate are used to produce the final output assuming a Leontief production function. With this technology, inputs are required in fixed proportions and thus there is no substitutability between the value-added and composite intermediates.[69] Each region participates in the trade with other regions. However, in this paper, the Cobb-Douglas production function will be substituted for the Leontief production function at the final stage. Fundamental equations are as follows,

$$Y_i = A_i \prod_{j=1}^{N} x_{ji} \, V_i$$

Where Y_i: Production output in sector I

x_{ji}: Composite intermediate input j in sector I

V_i: Value added in sector I

A_i: Constant parameter for technical efficiency

---

69) Hertel, T.W., ed (1997).

B. Demand Side

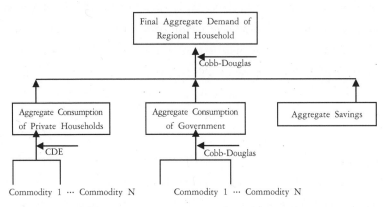

Figure V-3 Demand Structures of the GTAP Model

As shown in Figures V-3, regional household behavior is governed by an aggregate utility function, specified over composite private consumption, composite government purchases, and savings. The regional household utility function uses an index of current government expenditure to proxy the welfare derived from the government's provision of public goods and services to private households in the region. Here, the accounting relationships of the components of final demand are exhibited in an open economy. The "regional household" maximizes a Cobb-Douglas utility function constrained by a budget which is made up of the total tax revenue and endowment incomes of agents residing in this region. The utility maximization behavior forms demand equations, which are regarded as constant shares of the regional household income. Each region's disposable income is totally exhausted according to private households' consumption, government's spending and savings. The incorporation of the savings helps to capture the medium-run capital accumulation effect of policy reforms.

The utility from government spending approximates the welfare generated from the provision of public goods and services. The allocation of spending by the government across composite goods is based on a Cobb-Douglas utility function, while private household preferences are dictated by a constant difference of elasticities (CDE) implicit expenditure function. Imported commodities and domestically produced commodities are combined in a composite nest for both private and government expenditures, respectively. The elasticity of substitution between imported and domestically produced goods in this composite nest of the utility tree is assumed to be equal across uses. Import demand equations of firms and households therefore differ only in their import shares.

C. Government's Interruption and Value Linkage

Government's interruption works according to the taxes and subsidies. Due to tax and subsidy, there exist two prices in economic system: Market prices and Agent prices. And the whole value linkage can be demonstrated by figure V-4. VOM is equal to the aggregation of VOA and production Taxes. And the products will be consumed by three sectors by destination, domestic consumption (VDM), foreign consumption (VXMD) and an assumed transportation sector (VST). Here, the VST will decide the international transportation cost for the country. Now, after export tariff is added to or export subsidy is subtracted from VXMD, VXMD will become VXWD which is equal to the country's export price by FOB. When the transportation cost (VTWR) is added to VXWD, the value will become importing country's price by CIF. VIMS of the importing country will appear after import tariff is added to VIWS. All the imported products are aggregated together into a composite import product whose average price is defined as average import price, namely the composite products price facing the domestic consuming agents consisting of private agent (VIPM), government (VIGM) and firms (VIFM).

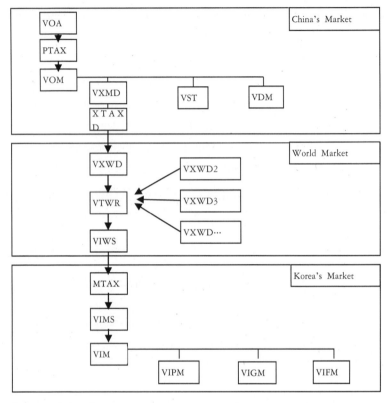

Figure V-4 Value Linkage

D. The Investment Determinations and the Closure for the Model

Having described the value linkage structure, it remains to discuss the model closure. Like most comparative static CGE models, the GTAP model does not account for monetary effects. Rather, the GTAP model is concerned with simulating the effects of trade policy and resource-related shocks on the medium-term patterns of global production and trade. Because this model is neither an inter-temporal model, nor sequenced through time to obtain a series of temporary equilibriums, investment does not come immediately in the next period to affect the productive capacity of regions in the model. But considering that a reallocation of investment across regions will affect production and trade through its impact on final demand, it is important to pay some attention to this. Also, a proper treatment of the savings-investment link is necessary in order to complete the global economic system, thereby assuring consistency in our accounting. Because there is no inter-temporal mechanism for determination of investment, we face a macroeconomic closure which includes an independent investment relationship and it simply accommodates any change in savings.

In addition to adopting a closure rule with respect to investment, it is necessary to deal with potential changes in the current account. In multi-region trade models, it is common to force domestic savings and investment to move with each other according to fixing the current account balance. To understand this, it is useful to pursue the accounting identity as follows,

$$S - I = X - M$$

This formula states that the national savings (S) minus investment (I) is identically equal to the current account surplus. By fixing the right-hand side of identity, the difference between national savings and investment is also fixed. This may be accomplished in the GTAP framework by fixing the trade balance and freeing up either national savings or investment.

If global savings equals global investment in the initial equilibrium, then the summation over the left-hand side of equation equals zero and the sum of all current account balances must initially be zero. Furthermore, by fixing the right-hand side of the equation on a regional basis, each region's share in the global pool of net savings is fixed. In this way, equality of global savings and investment in the new equilibrium is also assured, in spite of the fact that there is no "global bank" to mediate formally between savings and investment on a global basis. Finally, since investment is forced to adjust in line with regional changes in savings, this approach clearly falls within the "neoclassical" closure.[70)]

1.3. Existing Research on Korea-China FTA Using CGE Models

There has been research conducted by some scholars on a possible CK-FTA. Depending on differing scenarios and prerequisites, they hauled in different research results or predictions related to some macroeconomic effects on GDP, welfare, import-export, and so on from projected CK-FTA scenarios.

Outstanding work by the scholars of the Korea Institute for international Economic Policy (KIEP) reveals the potential effects of a KC FTA by

---

70) Thomas W. Hertel and Marinos E. Tsigas, 1997, p53.

using two CGE models. One is a static CGE model that captures the short-run effects and the other captures the static effects as well as the capital accumulation effects arising from higher savings and investment induced by the static reaps. They have set two simulation scenarios which involve the full elimination of tariffs in agricultural and manufactured goods (Scenario I) and the elimination of tariff and non-tariff barriers in agriculture and manufactured goods and the reduction in trade barriers in services by 50 percent (Scenario II). Outcomes have been calculated as follows,

Table V-2 The Effects of a Korea-China FTA Unit (%)

	Scenario I	GDP	Welfare	Export	Import	ToT
The Effects of a Korea-China FTA (Static Model)	Korea	2.443	1.132	4.756	5.152	1.235
	China	0.395	0.073	3.537	4.732	0.154
	Scenario II					
	Korea	2.472	1.164	4.787	5.182	1.237
	China	0.401	0.084	3.561	4.763	0.154
The Effects of a Korea-China FTA (Capital Model)	Scenario I	GDP	Welfare	Export	Import	ToT
	Korea	3.132	2.989	5.433	5.858	0.942
	China	0.584	0.593	3.733	4.944	0.128
	Scenario II					
	Korea	3.174	3.03	5.477	5.903	0.939
	China	0.594	0.603	3.862	4.98	0.127

Source: Hongshik Lee, Hyejoon Lm, Inkoo Lee, Backhoon Song, Soonchan Park of KIEP

The basic KIEP rationale for their government and industry-funded work can be found in the following key statements, "Traditional trade theory suggests that the formation of an FTA will lead to an increase in GDP via the increased efficiency of resource allocation. Trade liberalization induces resources to move from industries with comparative disadvantages to industries with comparative advantages. New trade theory based on economies of scale addresses the pro-competitive effects that result from the interactions between imperfect competition and trade liberalization. An FTA leads to a weakening of domestic firms' dominant positions in their home markets. In addition, the expansion of the market through integration provides an opportunity to increase sales in the export market."[71]

Based on neoclassical growth theory, Baldwin indicates that the static efficiency gain will be multiplied into a medium-run growth bonus, which induces higher savings and investments. New growth theory suggests that an FTA will have a positive effect on economic growth if it spurs the accumulation of human or knowledge capital (Baldwin 1989, 1992). KIEP research indicated early that the effects of a CK-FTA on GDP and welfare of the two countries arise from a mixture of terms-of-trade (ToT) and efficiency gains from resource allocation. Table V-2 presents the economy-wide effects of a CK-FTA according to the scenarios on the assumption of fixed capital. These involve changes in GDP, welfare, terms of trade, aggregated exports and imports. Table V-3 also presents that trade between Korea and China will increase greatly due to trade diversion caused by the establishment of the FTA. Without doubt, all results are quite positive fundamentals to the effects of a CK-FTA on both countries.

---

71) Hongshik Lee, Hyejoon Lm, Inkoo Lee, Backhoon Song, Soonchan Park.(2005) "Economic Effects of a Korea-China FTA and Policy Implications". Published December 30, 2005 in Korea by KIEP.

Table V-3 Changes in the Trade Volume among Countries (Unit: million dollars)

To/From	Static model (Scenario I)			Capital accumulation model (Scenario II)		
	Korea	China	Others	Korea	China	Others
Korea		14,219.90	-7,151.60		14,545.70	-6,343.00
China	13,998.10		-1,211.70	14,501.10		-960.4
Others	-6,912.70	-947.6	4,004.70	-5,563.40	-225.1	4,215.80
Total	7,085.40	13,272.30	-4,358.60	8,937.70	14,320.60	-3,087.60

Source: Hongshik Lee, Hyejoon Lm, Inkoo Lee, Backhoon Song, Soonchan Park of KIEP

Another insight has been offered by Chinese scholar Zhang Jianping from China Development Research Center of State Council (DRC). He has used partial CGE model to reflect on quantitative analysis of the of a CK FTA's influence. He created the partial equilibrium model (PEM), which focuses on the effects of the price of and demand for the imported products under the conditions of tariff reduction. An FTA signed by China and Korea would have both countries reduce tariffs and abolish non-tariff barriers, which probably would cause trade creation and trade diversion in the short term. While trade creation is mainly focused on the positive effects for Korea brought about by an FTA, the trade diversion effect mainly considers the negative properties on other countries in the global multilateral system caused by a bilateral CK-TA.

Zhang's research proved a CK FTA would bring obvious economic effects. First, in the short term, zero tariffs on China's imports from Korea would result in considerable trade creation effects, with a total value of about $2.42 billion, which corresponds to 5.6 percent of China's imports from Korea in 2003. In most industries, the trade creation values equal 5-15 percent of China's import from Korea in 2003. Second, for those industries for which the import value from Korea is quite large, such as machinery and electronic equipment (item 16), plastic (item 7), textiles (item 11), base metals (item 15), optics (item 18), mineral products (item 5), etc., their trade creation values would be higher than other industries and surpass $100 million. The trade creation value on machines and electronics is over $540 million, and for food and tobacco the trade creation proportion on total imports from Korea is over 30 percent. Third, a CK FTA would not influence other countries while the total trade diversion value is about $1.68 billion which is equal to 0.5 percent of other countries exports to China, as well as the 3.9 percent of Korea's exports to China.[72]

1.4. Model Aggregation for a Korea-China FTA

Microeconomic closure is adopted to reflect the choice of time frame. It is important to emphasize again that the time frame element can't be interpreted in terms of calendar years, but rather in terms of the adjustments that are allowed to take place in the (unobservable) transition to a new equilibrium. A neoclassical approach is adopted-fixing the endowments of productive factors and allowing market prices to adjust to maintain full employment.

This type of closure is often interpreted as representing the medium run, since it envisages a situation where the existing capital stock is able to move between sectors in response to variations in the rates of return to capital across sectors. However, the period considered is not long enough for new investment to come online as productive capital.

---

72) Zhang Jianping, "Analysis on the Issues of and Prospects for a China-Korea FTA". CNAEC Research Series 06-04, 2006.

The Closure used here is the standard GTAP model closure. Global investment is assumed to be responsive to changes in the relative rates of return across regions. This does not affect productive capital stocks but does have an impact on saving and thus on the current account balance in each region.

Table V-4 Model Aggregations

Regions	Sectors		Factors
China South Korea Japan NAFTA(3 Countries) EU(15 Countries) ASEAN(6 countries) Rest of World	1	Rice	
	2	Other Crops	
	3	Other food products	
	4	Animals and meat	
	5	Forestry	
	6	Fishing	
	7	Petrol, coal, gas and oil	
	8	Minerals	
	9	Beverages and tobacco products	Land
	10	Textiles, Apparel and leather products	Labor Force
	11	Wood and paper products	Capital
	12	Chemicals	
	13	Metals	
	14	Transport equipment, Motor vehicles	
	15	Electronic equipment	
	16	Other manufactures	
	17	Trade and business service	
	18	Transportation, communication service	
	19	Finance and insurance	
	20	Other service	

Source: aggregated by author

For this investigation, seven regions and twenty product sectors are distinguished in the model aggregations. The choice of regional dimension is motivated by primary focus on China, Korea, Japan, EU, NAFTA, and ASEAN with the other countries in ROW. For sector aggregation, 20 composite clusters are considered. Refer to Table V-4 for the details of regional and sectoral aggregations. In each region, there are 3 other agents, which are firm, private household and the government. GTAP determines regional supplies of and demands for goods and services through optimizing behavior of agents in competitive markets. Optimizing behaviors also determine sector demands for primary factors, such as labor, capital, land and natural resources. In each region there are two types of labor, skilled and unskilled, and single, homogenous capital goods. But in this constellation, the two types of labors are integrated into one. In standard comparative static application of the model, total supplies of capital, labor, land and natural resources are fixed for each region.

Table V-5 Bilateral Import Protection Levels per Sector

Sectors \ Tariff Rate	Bilateral Import Tariff Rate	
	Korea's Tariff Rate (%)	China's Tariff Rate (%)
Rice(1)	1000.0	0.7
Other Crops(2)	337.4	4.1
Other food products(3)	41.0	14.1
Animals and meat(4)	20.1	11.9
Forestry(5)	4.0	8.1
Fishing(6)	15.4	13.4
Petrol, coal, gas and oil(7)	2.2	7.0
Minerals(8)	6.4	12.3
Beverages and tobacco(9)	50.2	23.3
Textiles, Apparel and leather(10)	10.7	16.5
Wood and paper(11)	5.4	12.9
Chemicals(12)	7.1	11.4
Metals(13)	4.5	8.0
Transportation(14)	6.9	37.6
Electronic equipment(15)	2.5	9.0
Other manufactures(16)	6.8	12.9
Trade and business service(17)	No data	No data
Transportation Communication(18)	No data	No data
Finance and insurance(19)	No data	No data
Other service(20)	No data	No data
Total	1520.5670	203.0922

Source: GTAP Data 6.0

In my analysis, KC FTA is simulated under two alternative scenarios. In full scenario, all tariffs in food and manufactures between China and Korea are assumed to remove on a preferential basis. In partial scenario, depending on the bilateral tariff rates between Korea and China and their respective sensitive sectors, (see table V-5), Korea's rice will be excluded from tariff elimination and 50% of its import tariff from China in other crops will be removed. Remaining import tariffs from China to Korea are cut to zero; On the Chinese side, China's transport equipment and other manufactures will be excluded from tariff elimination while 50% of China's import tariff from Korea in Electronic equipment will be eliminated. Then all of China's other import tariffs from Korea are eliminated.

02 | The China-Korea FTA's Potential Economic Impact

2.1. Economic Effects on Welfare

The welfare measure used in the results is the equivalent variation (EV) for each regional household, expressed in millions of US dollars. The national welfare is measured by EV in income. EV in income is the amount of money that would have to be taken away from the consumer before the price change to leave her/him as well off as he/she would be after the price change. In other words, EV measures the maximum amount of income the consumer is willing to pay to avoid the price change. Therefore, EV can be interpreted as the change in regional household income at constant prices that is equivalent to the proposed change. Since EV uses beginning-period prices as its base, welfare results from alternative simulations can be directly compared. To offer an idea of the magnitude of the welfare gains, I have also expressed them as a percentage of initial regional GDP. These figures are presented in Tables V-6 and V-7, respectively. The GTAP system separates prices and quantities in the database by assuming initial prices equal to unity. Since the data values are expressed in millions of dollars, the quantity unit for volume changes in each region is the amount that would have been sold in the initial equilibrium for $1 million. It is necessary to consider the initial level of trade or the changed volume of GDP. In some instances, for example, large percentage changes merely reflect very small initial trade levels.

Table V-6 Welfare Effect of a Korea-China FTA in two Scenarios

EV / Region	(1) Partial Tariff Elimination (Million US Dollars)	(2) Full Tariff Elimination (Million US Dollars)
China	227	1057
Korea	5691	15522
Japan	-399	78
NAFTA	-956	-1788
EU	-311	-511
ASEAN	-308	-385
Rest of World	-1383	-1836

Source: model simulations by author
Note: (mean equivalent variation, millions of US Dollars)

The results indicate that both Korea and China would benefit in welfare in two scenarios while the gains are quite different between the two economies in two scenarios. From the simulation results, in partial scenario, Korea's welfare would increase greatly with 5691 million US dollars, while China's welfare is just expected to increase 227 million US dollars. In full scenario, due to the more liberalization in all sectors, both of the welfare values are expected to increase. Korea's welfare will increase greatly with 15522 million US dollars, three times larger than the value in partial one. China's welfare is expected to increase 1057 million US dollars with a leap expected to be more than six times as high as in the partial.

Table V-7 Real GDP Changes from a China-Korea FTA in two Scenarios

GDP / Region	(1) Partial Tariff Elimination (Percentage change %)	(2) Full Tariff Elimination (Percentage change %)
China	0.052	0.052
Korea	0.728	3.065
Japan	-0.002	0.005
NAFTA	0.001	0.001
EU	0.000	0.001
ASEAN	-0.009	-0.003
ROW	-0.005	-0.006

Source: model simulations by author

Table V-8 Effect of China-Korea FTA on Real GDP in two Scenarios

GDP / Region	(1) Partial Tariff Elimination (Million US Dollars)	(2) Full Tariff Elimination (Million US Dollars)
China	687	689
Korea	3112	13108
Japan	-62	219
NAFTA	51	78
EU	25	110
ASEAN	-44	-13
ROW	-249	-307

Source: model simulations by author

As to the variation in two countries' GDP in partial scenario, Korea's real GDP is expected to increase by 0.73 percent with 3112 million US dollars increase, However, China's real GDP only increases by 0.05 percent with a smaller change. In full scenario, China's real GDP has almost no increase compared to the partial scenario, ether in absolute or in relative terms (See table V-6, V-7 and V-8). But Korea's real GDP is expected to increase sharply by 3.06 percent which is more than four times greater than the value under the partial scenario.

On the other hand, we also have quite clear evidence of the negative effects on welfare in non-member countries. An important result is that virtually all other economies in the model are estimated to lose their welfares under two scenarios-except Japan's welfare change in the full scenario. The most substantial welfare losses are to NAFTA in the EV and to ASEAN in proportional terms of the GDP (except ROW). This result indicates the presence of trade diversion effects and the declines in the terms-of-trade of nonmember economies associated with the switching of imports to preferential trading partner sources.

Table V-9 Decomposition of Welfare Effect of Korea-China FTA on China and Korea

EV Region	Allocative Efficiency		Changes in Terms of Trade		Changes in Investment-Savings		Total Changes of EV_ALT	
	Partial	Full	Partial	Full	Partial	Full	Partial	Full
China	687	689	-565	173	29	35	151	897
Korea	3114	13055	2375	2046	-408	-524	5081	14578

Source: model simulations by author
Note: welfare refers to EV_ALT (regional EV computed in alternative way)
Unit: million US dollars

Table V-10 Effects on Korea and China's Allocative Efficiency

	Allocative Efficiency Effects									
AEE Region	Change in production		Change in Consumption		Change in exports		Change in imports		Total Change in AEE	
	Partial	Full	Partial	Full	Partial	Full	Partial	Full	Partial	Full
China	234.1	67.4	-4.7	-10.0	77.1	-2.5	380.0	634.1	687	689
Korea	115.0	1052.1	461.6	584.3	-12.9	-61.5	2550.2	11480.4	3114	13055

Source: model simulations by author
Unit: million us dollars

Allocative efficiency is the market condition whereby resources are allocated in a way that maximizes the net benefits through their use. Allocative efficiency implies a situation where the limited resources of a country are allocated in accordance with the wishes of consumers. An allocatively efficient economy produces an "optimal mix" of commodities. A firm is allocatively efficient when its price is equal to its marginal cost in a perfect market. From table V-10, we can see, two countries' Allocative Efficiency will increase quickly in two scenarios, which reflects the improvements of the economic efficiency in both countries. In other words, the welfare results estimated in the scenarios reflect the benefits of reallocation of resources in and between China and Korea.

Table V-9 and V-10 reveal the sources of gains from an FTA between Korea and China. Not surprisingly, the welfare gains probably derive from different effects in the two economies. The sources of welfare gains for the two countries are quite the same in the full scenario but different in the partial one. In the full scenario on the Chinese side, most of its welfare gains are from the changes of its import (634 million US Dollars) and the improvements in the terms of trade (173 million US Dollars). In the Korean case, most of its welfare gains are caused by the changes in Korean imports (11480.4 million US Dollars) and the improvements in terms of trade (2046.0 million US Dollars), which is quite similar to China's situation. In the partial scenario, China's gains mainly come from the changes of its imports (380 million US Dollars) and the increase of its production (234 million US Dollars) while its terms of trade become worse (-565 million US Dollars). Korean welfare gains are still mainly from the changes in its import (2550.2 million US Dollars) and its terms of trade (2374.8 million US Dollars) as behaviors in the full scenario.

These improvements reflect the two countries' benefits from potential CK-FTA. In China's case, terms-of-trade effects are negative in partial scenario, which reflects the costs associated with trade diversion. The largest gains for China come from improvements in allocative efficiency in imports. In Korea's case, in two scenarios, Korea's largest gains both come from the changes of its import and terms of trade, which constitute major Korean welfare gains. However, Korean investments and savings (IS) changes both reduce its welfare gains in two scenarios compared to China's small increase in this index. But generally speaking, compared to Korean changes in welfare and GDP in two scenarios, China's gains are relatively smaller.

Actually, in models, the effects of scale-economies that can exist under imperfect competition are not captured. Dynamic gains from investment effects will make all these respective indices much higher and more prominent. Moreover, because of limitations in the available data, service liberalization is not captured. For this reason, the results presented here are probably lower-bound estimates of the potential welfare effects of a CK-FTA.

2.2. Economic Effects of a China-Korea FTA on Trade

A. Effects on Korea and China's Total Imports and Exports

One key benefit from a CK-FTA is to have more secure access to the other market. This would be very important, particularly for Korea, since Korean exports to China make up 22.07 percent of its total exports which in turn represented 50 percent of the Korean GDP in 2007. This means that Korean exports to China contribute about 11 percent to its total GDP in 2007. Thus it is very important for Korea to secure its market access to China.

Table V-11 Effects on Imports by Region

Import Region	Import Changes by Region	
	Partial Scenario	Full Scenario
China	10828 (2.74)	16342 (4.13)
Korea	13139 (8.08)	25632 (15.77)
Japan	-576 (-0.14)	2 (0.00)
NAFTA	-1057 (-0.06)	-1909 (-0.11)
EU	-552 (-0.02)	-802 (-0.03)
ASEAN	-521 (-0.15)	-805 (-0.23)
Rest of World	-1969 (-0.13)	-2396 (-0.15)

Source: model simulations by author
Note: (units: million US dollars and percent change in parentheses respectively)

Table V-12 Effects on Exports by Region

Region \ Export	Export Changes by Region	
	Partial Tariff Elimination	Full Tariff Elimination
China	10454 (2.12)	15617 (3.16)
Korea	9425 (4.91)	19669 (10.25)
Japan	-47 (-0.01)	568 (0.12)
NAFTA	264 (0.02)	677 (0.05)
EU	-53 (0.00)	272 (0.01)
ASEAN	-260 (-0.06)	-461 (-0.11)
Rest of World	-547 (-0.03)	-454 (-0.03)

Source: model simulations by author
Note: (units: million US dollars and percent change in parentheses respectively)

Table V-11 gives the volume and percentage changes in total imports by region and Table V-12 shows the changes in total exports by region. The results indicate smaller changes for China in terms of its import and export percentage changes while Korea's imports and exports are expected to have large increases in terms of the percentage changes.

In partial scenario, China's imports and exports are expected to increase 2.74 percent and 2.12 percent while Korea's imports and exports are expected to increase greatly to 8.08 percent and 4.91 percent. When considering the changes of imports and exports in volume changes, more detailed results can be obtained. China's imports and exports are expected to increase 10828 and 10454 million US dollars and Korea's imports and exports are expected to increase 13139 and 9425 million US dollars, respectively. According to volume changes, I found the two countries' trade changes in either imports or exports are very close although there is a great difference in percentage variation between Korea and China.

In the full scenario, percentage changes of all corresponding variables are expected to increase drastically. China's imports and exports are expected to increase 4.13 percent and 3.16 percent and Korea's imports and exports are expected to increase 15.77 percent and 10.25 percent. The two countries' changes in trade in volume also follow this tendency accordingly. China's imports and exports are expected to increase 16342 and 15617 million US dollars, and Korea's imports and exports are expected to increase 25632 and 19669 million US dollars, respectively. Here, compared to the volume changes in partial scenario, China's imports and exports would increase 33.74 percent and 33.29 respectively and Korean imports and exports would increase 48.74 percent and 52.08 percent in the full scenario.

By the way, some of the increases in China's exports to Korea would come from the trade diversion of Japanese or other world regions' products imported into Korea. At the same time, some of the increases in Korean exports to China would come from trade diversion of imports from Japan or other regions. The regional exports and imports patterns in Table V-13 confirm the presence of trade diversion in trade. Considering non-member regions, the trade diversion can be easily found out. China increases its exports to Korea substantially, but its exports to all other regions fall due to the elimination of bilateral tariffs with Korea from the CK-FTA. Korea also increases its exports to China in a similar way. Under the partial and full scenario, imports of all other regions will suffer a decrease to some degree, except for Japan's import in the full scenario, and all the non-members' exports except for NAFTA are expected to decrease.

Table V-13 Impact on Bilateral Trade in Full Scenario (million US dollars)

	China	Japan	NAFTA	EU	ASEAN	ROW
Korea's Import	20259	1329	73	1093	310	1031
Korea's Export	32049	1472	-4360	-2248	-1371	-3805
	Korea	Japan	NAFTA	EU	ASEAN	ROW
China's Import	32049	-3079	-1607	-2355	-1849	-3568
China's Export	20259	-477	39	-293	-39	-334

Source: model simulations by author

However, in two scenarios, both Korea's exports and imports with Japan are expected to increase. Korea's imports from all the non-members are also expected to increase in the partial scenario. Actually, when Korean exports to China increase substantially (China's imports from Korea increase by definition), imports from other economies do not necessarily fall (see Table V-13). Expansion of China's income may result in import increases from Japan, NAFTA or the EU. Similarly, efficiency gains also seem to allow Korea to expand exports to non-member regions in some cases.

B. Effects on Korea and China's Imports and Exports by Sector

In the case of a CK-FTA, it is generally expected that the increase of China's exports to Korea in food sectors would exceed Korea's exports increases to China since China's trade barriers in food sectors currently are already low, that is, they are significantly lower than those of Korean. However, in manufacturing sectors, China's exports to Korea are expected to be less than the increase of Korean exports to China since China's trade barriers in manufacture sectors currently are relatively high and generally higher than those of Korean.

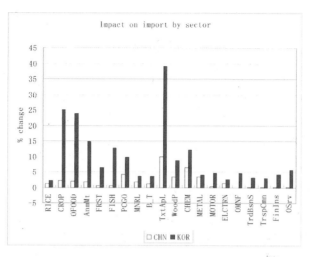

Source: made by author (percentage changes).

Figure V-5 Effects on Korea and China's Imports by Sector in Partial Scenario

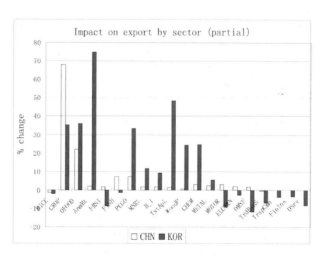

Source: made by author (percentage changes)

Figure V-6 Effects on Korea and China's Exports by Sector in Partial Scenario

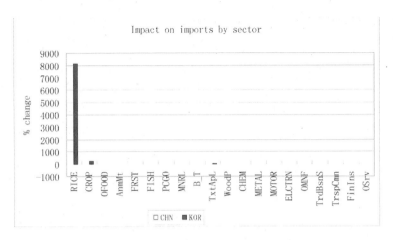

Source: made by author (percentage changes)

Figure V-7 Effects on Korea and China's Imports by Sector in Full Scenario

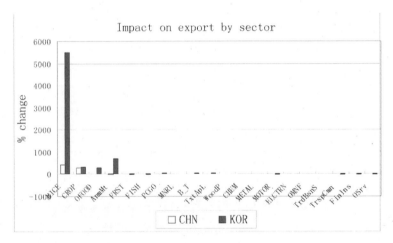

Source: made by author (percentage changes)

Figure V-8 Effects on Korea and China's Exports by Sector in Full Scenario

Changes of Imports and Exports by Sector in China

The changes in China's exports and imports arising from the FTA are indicated in Figures V-5 to V-8. China's imports in all sectors are expected to increase due to trade diversion and trade creation from within a CK-FTA. Under the partial scenario, China's imports in textiles, apparel, leather and chemicals are expected to have strong increase rates. Meanwhile, China's exports in crops and food products are expected to show sudden increase leaps. However, China's exports in rice are expected to decrease and the tariff eliminations in food and manufacture will lead to a trade reduction in China's service sectors.

Under the full scenario (please refer to V-7-1 and V-8-1 in the appendix), the changes in both import and export volumes are relatively larger for China. China's imports for rice, textiles, crops, animals, meat and chemicals are expected to earn high increase rates. There should be large increases in some agricultural exports when these goods are included in the FTA. The largest percentage changes are for rice and crops although they have a high degree of uncertainty since they come from a very small sector base. The differences between the changes of trade volumes, on the other hand, vary from the devises of different scenarios.

Changes of Imports and Exports by Sector in Korea

Turning to the Korean side of the agreement, Korea will gain more market shares as a result of an FTA. In most sectors, Korea's share of imports is more than one percent. Under the partial scenario, Korea's imports in textiles, crops and food products will increase. As I exclude rice and just eliminate 50 percent tariff for the Korean crops, Korean exports in rice are expected to decrease 2.17 percent, which reflects Korean weak competition in its rice sector. Under the full scenario, Korea's imports and exports in rice and crops will expand quickly, and Korea's exports in food products, animals, and meat are also expected to increase quickly. More detailed changes applicable to this area have been explained in references V-7-1 and V-8-1 in the appendix.

As analyzed, however, rice and crop products are both sensitive sectors for Korea. Therefore, even the export shares are expected to increase in these sectors. Considering the smaller original volume of its export in these sectors, these indices are mainly reflecting the increasing rates, which may explain why Korea's exports in these sectors before a CK-FTA would be very small. Even these sectors will earn rapid increases in their exports by percentage variation, while the real export volume probably would be small. In terms of limitations of the analysis framework, it should be noted that trade estimates tend to be highly dependent on the Armington elasticities. Also, the model is unable to capture "new" trade, but only expansions and contractions in existing trade. However, at this level of aggregation, this issue does not come into play.

C. Effects on Trade Balance

Table V-14 Impact on Trade Balance by Region (million US dollars)

Regions	Partial Tariff Elimination	Full Tariff Elimination
China	-957	-593
Korea	-1264	-3727
Japan	342	684
NAFTA	994	2014
EU	340	833
ASEAN	-17	-46
Rest of World	563	834

Source: model simulations by author

An FTA could also help ameliorate or worsen a balance of payments problem. Having trade discrimination and diversion as a result of an FTA may in fact be beneficial to FTA partner countries. The CK-FTA would have the effect of changing Korea and China's trade balance. FTA will cause the increases of both exports and imports for its member countries. Changes of trade balances for FTA members are mainly subject to their trade changes with their FTA partners. GTAP model simulations confirm both Korea and China's trade balance will deteriorate although the absolute volumes are not big enough due to a CK-FTA under two scenarios. Even if the net effect turns out to be negative, not only should it be small because of the negating effect of trade diversion on the trade balance. Contrarily, it could still be beneficial to Korea and China in terms of its mutually deepening and widening trade relations.

The results presented in Table V-14 reflect changes in trade balance (the value of exports at world price less the value of imports at world prices). Clearly, this chart is relevant only when the closure allows flexibility of the current account (otherwise it is zero by definition). The results indicate that the two countries' current account positions worsen under both scenarios. In the partial scenario, China and Korea's trade deficits would increase 957 million US dollars and 1264 million US dollars respectively. However, when all the bilateral import tariffs are removed in the full scenario, China's trade deficits would decrease while Korean trade deficits would increase to almost three times larger compared to its volume changes in the partial scenario.

Table V-15 Impact on Trade Balance by Region in Full Scenario (Million US Dollars)

	China	Japan	NAFTA	EU	ASEAN	ROW
Korea's Imports	20259	1329	73	1093	310	1031
Korea's Exports	32049	1472	-4360	-2248	-1371	-3805
Korea's Trade Balance	11790	142	-4433	-3342	-1681	-4836
	Korea	Japan	NAFTA	EU	ASEAN	ROW
China's Imports	32049	-3079	-1607	-2355	-1849	-3568
China's Exports	20259	-477	39	-293	-39	-334
China's Trade Balance	-11790	2602	1646	2062	1810	3234

Source: model simulations by author

The figures in table V-15 show the changes in bilateral trade balances caused by Korea-China FTA in full scenario, which are calculated on the same basis as the overall balance (that is, the value of exports at world prices less the value of imports at world prices, by region). Since only the overall current account balance is constrained in closure, the bilateral balances can always vary. Korea has often been under trade pressure from China because of its chronic and big trade surplus with China. On the other hand, Korea has had a severe trade deficit with Japan. In fact, Korea even tried to artificially divert imports from Japan to other countries under the "import source diversification system" for many years, but the effects are not evident. Theoretically speaking, An FTA with China could enable Korea to "naturally" divert imports from Japan to China, thereby mitigating the problem of trade imbalances with China and Japan.

The regional bilateral trade decomposition indicates improvement in the bilateral balance between Korea and China and deterioration between China and Korea (see Table V-15). The CK-FTA will continue to improve Korea's trade with China, which means the trade imbalance between China and Korea will become even more serious. Improvement in the

Korean bilateral trade balance with China tends to be offset by deterioration in bilateral balances with other economies such as NAFTA, EU, ASEAN and ROW. Korea's imports from Japan would not decrease while it expands its imports from China largely, and its exports with Japan also share such a tendency. Comparing the trade changes between Korea and Japan, the CK-FTA will help Korea improve its trade imbalance with Japan. But Korea's trade balance with NAFTA, EU, ASEAN and ROW are expected to become deteriorated. Caution needs to be taken in evaluating both the overall and bilateral balances, since the former is determined largely by saving behavior in the domestic economy, and the latter may not have a strong economic meaning.

Table V-16 Impact on Trade Balance by Sectors in Full Scenario
(Million US Dollars)

Sectors / Bilateral Trade	Changes of China's Exports to Korea	Changes of China's Imports from Korea	Changes of China's Trade Balance
Rice	2783	45	2738
Other Crops	8375	150	8224
Other food products	1218	875	343
Animals and meat	108	556	-449
Forestry	3	0	3
Fishing	45	1	44
Petrol, coal, gas and oil	494	1575	-1081
Minerals	213	244	-31
Beverages and tobacco	23	37	-14
Textiles, Apparel	2913	9336	-6423
Wood and paper	144	700	-556
Chemicals	716	5415	-4698
Metals	491	1253	-762
Transport	267	1879	-1611
Electronic equipment	855	5619	-4764
Other manufactures	1515	4405	-2890

Trade and business service	57	-3	60
Transport Communication	7	-9	16
Finance and insurance	27	-15	41
Other service	6	-14	20

Source: model simulations by author

As for the bilateral trade from the sectors' perspective (see Table V-16) in the full scenario, China could earn trade surplus with Korean trade in food or agricultural sectors such as rice, crops etc. However, China would suffer trade deficits in its manufacturing sectors such as chemical, transportation, and manufactures and so on. These results are quite consistent with my previous research empirically proving that China has relative competitive advantages in its agricultural fields while Korea has relative competitive advantages for its manufactures.

2.3. Economic Effects of a China-Korea FTA on Outputs

Table V-17 China and Korea's Outputs by Sector in Base Year

Output Sector	China (Volume)	Shares (%)	Korea (Volume)	Shares (%)
Rice(1)	44441	1.25	14086	1.45
Other Crops(2)	30171	0.85	3781	0.39
Other food products(3)	219020	6.18	32284	3.33
Animals and meat(4)	116828	3.29	11982	1.24
Forestry(5)	17464	0.49	744	0.08
Fishing(6)	27852	0.79	2425	0.25
Petrol, coal, gas and oil(7)	97794	2.76	25416	2.62
Minerals(8)	204316	5.76	13074	1.35
Beverages and tobacco(9)	50469	1.42	8328	0.86
Textiles, Apparel and leather(10)	294212	8.30	34838	3.59
Wood and paper(11)	100321	2.83	20317	2.10

Chemicals(12)	222993	6.29	64855	6.69
Metals(13)	221597	6.25	56007	5.78
Transportation(14)	85000	2.40	55452	5.72
Electronic equipment(15)	129175	3.64	69282	7.15
Other manufactures(16)	371797	10.49	80670	8.32
Trade and business service(17)	389324	10.98	128910	13.30
Transportation Communication(18)	141215	3.98	24933	2.57
Finance and insurance(19)	146163	4.12	81148	8.37
Other service(20)	635781	17.93	240954	24.85

Source: GTAP model and author's calculations
Note: volume unit, million US dollars

The changes in trade flows have different impacts on output at the sectoral and aggregate level in both countries. Generally speaking, an increased incentive for exports in one sector would increase its output. On the other hand, increased competition will take the form of a higher volume of imports and it may shrink domestic production in the sector, at least in a short term.

In a measure similar to that used for the trade figures, the changes in sectoral outputs for both economies are shown in table V-18 as percentage changes of output volumes relative to the initial output levels (see table V-17). They indicate very small structural effects on China's economy while there are larger impacts on Korean outputs.

Table V-18 Changes in Sectoral Outputs (Volume unit: million US dollars)

Sectors \ Output	China				Korea			
	Partial		Full		Partial		Full	
	%	Volume	%	Volume	%	Volume	%	Volume
Rice	-0.01	-4	7.79	3462	0.92	130	-36.89	-5196
Other Crops	6.15	1856	25.78	7778	-15.83	-599	-35.11	-1328
Other food products	0.81	1774	-0.29	-635	4.68	1511	47.60	15367
Animals and meat	-0.31	-362	-1.30	-1519	5.80	695	45.25	5422
Forestry	-0.05	-9	-0.03	-5	-2.69	-20	-3.27	-24
Fishing	0.26	72	0.81	226	-1.28	-31	2.44	59
Petrol, coal, gas and oil	0.39	381	0.44	430	10.56	2684	12.15	3088
Minerals	0.22	449	0.14	286	0.93	122	1.13	148
Beverages and tobacco	0.00	0	-0.15	-76	2.49	207	11.09	924
Textiles, Apparel ,leather	-1.08	-3177	-1.75	-5149	30.54	10640	27.99	9751
Wood and paper	-0.04	-40	-0.38	-381	4.33	880	4.90	996
Chemicals	0.01	22	0.19	424	10.53	6829	12.43	8061
Metals	0.32	709	-0.04	-89	-0.88	-493	-1.71	-958
Transportations	0.57	485	-0.28	-238	-5.71	-3166	-3.35	-1858
Electronic equipment	1.30	1679	1.42	1834	-2.62	-1815	-0.23	-159
Other manufactures	0.76	2826	-0.05	-186	-6.25	-5042	-0.19	-153
Trade and business service	-0.04	-156	-0.14	-545	0.48	619	4.47	5762
Transport, Communication	0.02	28	0.02	28	-0.47	-117	-0.19	-47
Finance and insurance	0.04	58	0.03	44	-0.05	-41	0.48	390
Other service	0.08	509	0.11	699	1.13	2723	2.94	7084

Source: model simulations by author

■ Changes in Sectoral Outputs in China

Analysis with regards to a partial agreement for China shows an overall increase across the food sectors and manufacture factors except a few, with the largest increase in other manufactures, followed by other crops, food products, and electronic equipment. These industries are expected to expand by 2.8 billion US dollars, 1.8 billion US dollars,

1.8 billion US dollars and 1.7 billion US dollars, respectively. Other industries, which show a relatively large increase in production, are metals and other services. Here output is expected to increase by 0.32 percent and 0.08 percent, respectively. The contracting industries can be found within some manufacturing and service sectors. The largest drop in output could be found in China's textiles, apparel and leather, with a decrease by -1.08 percent (-3.1 billion US dollars), where ex-ante China's trade barrier was higher than its Korean counterpart. China's animal and meat also show a contraction of output, corresponding to -0.31 percent (-362 million US dollars). But the overall effect on China's economy is positive, since output share in increased industries is much larger in the overall output, whereby China's total economic output would increase by 7100 million US dollars.

In the full scenario, I still find big increases of China's outputs in other crops and electronic equipment. Here, these sectors are expected to increase by 25.78 percent (7. 8 billion US dollars) and 1.42 percent (1.8 billion US dollars), respectively. A sharp increase in China's rice output is also found, namely by 7.79 percent, which is quite different from the situation in the partial scenario and corresponds with the construction of the scenarios (I eliminated the bilateral import tariff for rice in full, except Korean rice in partial). The output changes differently in other manufacture sectors, transportation, and other crops sectors, reminding us that all these sectors' output changes reflect the tariff elimination differences between full and partial experimental policies. Besides these sectors, which respond sensitively to the artificial tariff devise, compared to the output in the partial scenario, the output in chemicals and fishing would increase much more while the output in other food products, beverages, and tobacco would decrease (see Table V-18).

■ Changes in Sectoral Outputs in Korea

As for the Korean side, Korean largest output increase, in partial scenario, would occur in textiles, apparel, and leather sector (30.54%), which is just expected to be China's biggest output contraction in the same scenario. Korean chemicals and energy sources are also expected to increase quickly, with a 10.53 and 2.49 percent expansion respectively. On the contrary, a picture emerges where there is a sharp contraction in transportation, electronic equipment, and other manufactures, decreasing by -5.71, -2.62 and -6.25 percent. The elimination of the bilateral tariffs in three of China's import tariff protections needs to be kept in mind for the partial scenario, whereby it becomes much easier to explain these results.

In the full scenario, Korean rice and other crops would decrease quickly due to Korea's weak comparative competition in agriculture. The output contraction in transportation, electronic equipment, and other manufactures still would continue, but the volumes are expected to be much smaller. On the expanding side, I find that as a result of more trade liberalization measures, the output in beverages and tobacco would increase four-fold of that in the partial scenario, while fishing would increase by 59 million US dollars from -31 million US dollars in the partial scenario. Interestingly, the output in Korea's other food products would expect to increase also by 10 times of the volume in the partial scenario too, which traditionally is not a strong industry in Korea.

Because of the lack of service data, the simulation results cannot reflect the real variation in both countries' service sectors. Theoretically speaking, the tariff elimination in food and manufacture sectors may reduce the output in service sectors due to the diversion of labor and capital to the food and manufacturing sectors but this feature does not occur except in China's trade and business services.

2.4. Effects of a China-Korea FTA on Demand Changes for Production Factors

An FTA will generally lead to the changes of productive incentives in a particular sector due to the variation of the competitive circumstance. Then productive resources are reallocated across sectors, and cross-sectoral demands for different production factors are altered. Because the supply of production factors is constrained at any given time, expansion of one sector usually means contraction in another. Generally speaking, membership in the CK-FTA has implications for almost all parts of the economy with production factors expanding in some sectors while contracting in others.

The effects of the CK-FTA on sectoral outputs would engender small changes in the demand for labor and capital in China and Korea. Simulation results indicate that for most sectors, the impact of the FTA on the demand changes for labor and capital would have synchronous directions in both countries in two scenarios (Table V-19), which means while the labor demand increases, the capital demand will also increase, and vice versa. Without considering the changes in technological development, changes in the demand for the different production factors should be closely related to the changes of outputs. It is, therefore, not surprising that the demands for labor and capital, in general, tend to be very similar to the impact on sectoral outputs reported earlier.

Table V-19 Effects on Demand Changes for Production Factors by Sector

Scenario / Sector	China				Korea			
	Partial		Full		Partial		Full	
	Labor	Capital	Labor	Capital	Labor	Capital	Labor	Capita
Rice	-0.16	-0.12	7.69	7.81	-0.22	-0.18	-63.42	-63.51
Other Crops	5.67	5.68	24.16	24.23	-16.06	-16.04	-38.12	-38.19
Other food products	0.80	0.85	-0.12	0.04	-3.48	-3.42	4.40	4.05
Animals and meat	-0.19	-0.15	-0.66	-0.52	0.61	0.66	9.80	9.49
Forestry	-0.13	-0.12	-0.15	-0.10	-3.03	-3.02	-5.81	-5.90
Fishing	0.21	0.22	0.78	0.83	-2.45	-2.43	-0.13	-0.22
Petrol, coal, gas and oil	0.04	0.06	-0.02	0.06	7.68	7.71	6.89	6.73
Minerals	-0.02	0.04	-0.25	-0.03	0.05	0.13	-0.38	-0.83
Beverages and tobacco	-0.13	-0.05	-0.20	0.06	-1.33	-1.23	-4.31	-4.81
Textiles, Apparel	-1.62	-1.54	-2.33	-2.05	27.25	27.39	23.26	22.54
Wood and paper	-0.35	-0.27	-0.79	-0.50	3.04	3.15	2.58	1.98
Chemicals	-0.46	-0.38	-0.42	-0.13	8.62	8.74	8.39	7.76
Metals	0.02	0.11	-0.51	-0.22	-2.22	-2.12	-3.80	-4.36
Transport	0.29	0.38	-0.87	-0.58	-6.89	-6.79	-5.41	-5.96
Electronic equipment	0.87	0.95	0.56	0.85	-4.31	-4.21	-3.05	-3.62
Other manufactures	0.44	0.53	-0.58	-0.29	-7.39	-7.29	-2.19	-2.76
Trade and business service	-0.22	-0.11	-0.48	-0.14	-0.44	-0.32	0.37	-0.33
Transport Communication	-0.17	-0.06	-0.40	-0.02	-1.12	-0.98	-1.20	-1.97
Finance and insurance	-0.14	-0.05	-0.38	-0.08	-0.80	-0.69	-0.76	-1.36
Other service	-0.13	-0.04	-0.27	0.03	0.48	0.58	1.48	0.88

Source: model simulations by author (percentage changes)

In the partial scenario, China's sectoral demands for labor and capital in China would increase in other crops, food products, fishing, and electronic equipment and so on, with the largest relative increase in other crops (5.67% in labor and 5.68% in capital), which is correspondent to the sector's output increase (6.15%), being the largest percentage change in output. Demands changes for both labor and capital follow the same variations as output changes in the full scenario for China. But the changed levels in all sectors would rise. There are four sectors (other food products; petrol, coal, gas and oil; beverages and tobacco and other service) whose demand changes in labor and capital are discordant in the full scenario while such a result can be found just in minerals in the partial scenario.

On the Korean side in the partial scenario, sectoral demands for labor and capital increase in animals, meat, petrol, coal, gas, oil, minerals, textiles, apparel, chemicals, wood, paper, and other materials. The demands for labor and capital in most of the other sectors would decrease. Compared to the results in the full scenario, I conclude with the following remarks.

First, the demand changes for labor and capital in each sector (except for trade and business services in the full scenario) are expected to move simultaneously into a similar direction, which means when labor demand increases, capital will also increase. Second, the demand changes for both labor and capital in each sector correspond with their output changes in the two scenarios. When sector output shows a general increase, demands for capital and labor will follow to increase. Third, the demand changes for both labor and capital in each sector are basically expected to keep a synchronous movement between the two scenarios (except for minerals and other food products).

CHAPTER

6

Conclusions

01 | Summary

This dissertation mainly explores the feasibility and potential economic effects of a CK-FTA. The research of both China and Korea's FTA strategies generalized their FTA polices and elaborate their FTA motives, which is followed by empirically expounding their trade relations, trade features and trade structures via normalized economic indices to reveal the respective advantage and disadvantages among different industries. Together with the related FTA theories, a systematic analysis on a CK-FTA's effects is exposed in the latter sections.

Under general conditions, a China-Korea FTA will bring benefits and advantages to both sides. In the Korean side, a CK-FTA will allow it easier to be accessible to a huge market of the Chinese economy, which will in turn improve Korea's balance of trade. In addition, it is expected the economic growth of China through a high degree of specialization of industry structures and efficiency-improvement in investments toward China can play an important role in Korea's economic growth. On the other side, China also can benefit much for the technology spillover from Korea's side due to the much closer economic relationship between

Korea and China.

However, people can never consider its prospects too optimistic, since CK-FTA's possible side effects. As the simulation results show, if the tariffs elimination process were completed overnight, the sensitive sectors in both countries would be severely attacked. In a sense, whether a CK-FTA would actually improve bilateral welfare or bring comprehensive merits to both countries will, to a great degree, depend on the CK-FTA experiment policies, which means the effects from a CK-FTA, will essentially rely on what kind of an ultimate FTA will be established.

The quantitative effects of an FTA were analyzed by using static CGE models under two experiment policies. One is a CGE model that captures the short-term effects in partial tariff elimination while the other scenario considers full bilateral import tariff eliminations. In partial scenario one, it has been estimated that the net welfare of China and Korea will increase by 227 and 5691 million US dollars respectively, due to resource reallocation to sectors where comparative advantages exist. The same volumes will increase to 1.06 and 15.52 billion US dollars respectively in a full scenario. And the two countries' "Allocative Efficiency" (AE) will increase quickly in two scenarios, which reflect the improvements of the economic efficiency in both countries, while China's AE indicators such as the changes in consumption and import are much smaller than Korea's perspective, as reflects much higher growth rates of Korea's welfare.

Bilateral exports and imports would change greatly during trade diversion and trade creation from the elimination of the bilateral import tariffs. In a partial scenario, China's exports and imports are expected to grow

10.45 (2.12%) and 10.83 (2.74%) billion US dollars respectively, and its export and imports would increase by 15.62 (3.16%) and 16.34 (4.13%) billion US dollars in a full scenario. Therefore, under the two scenarios, China is expected to suffer a greater trade deficit. On the Korean side, exports and imports are also expected to increase quickly, with 9.43 (4.91%) and 13.14 (8.07%) billion US dollars in the partial scenario, and 19.67 (10.25%) and 25.63 (15.77%) billion US dollars respectively in the full scenario. On the other hand, trade changes in different sectors are expected to experience different changes. Exports in sectors which have relative competitive advantages would expand while the exports in sectors without competitive advantages would diminish. As to the trade balance changes, the two countries' total trade balances are expected to become worse. And the CK-FTA is expected to improve Korea's trade balance to China but deteriorate China's trade balance to Korea. Sector output changes and production factor movement would vary depending on their competitive advantages.

In conclusion, a CK-FTA has many positive economic impacts and generously would bring mutual benefits, such as the increases in welfare, trade volume, and potential overall economic growth. At this point, it could be so bold as to predict that a CK-FTA would provide a new impetus for the two countries' prospective economic growth. However, FTA side effects are also exposed from the simulation results. Both countries' relatively competitive industries will be better off while other relatively less competitive sectors will be worse off. If CK-FTA's scenario is not devised in a reciprocal way, either of the countries probably would suffer more than expected. For example, along with the reallocations of industrial structure in the two countries, the unemployment rate in less competitive industries, at least in the short run, would increase to cause possible seriously social problems. In sensitive sectors, Korea has to focus on the protection of its agricultural industries, especially in its rice, other crops, even in some labor intensive industries. China should improve its competition in its manufacture industries, such as its electronic equipment and chemicals, to enhance the competitiveness of these industries together with the adjustment of industrial structure.

On company levels, the positive benefits of FTA are expected to increase effectiveness through expanding the market and encouraging competitiveness. A CK-FTA would provide the two countries' companies with distinct opportunity to work and invest with each other. Some companies will develop benefits from the CK-FTA while uncompetitive companies will be naturally removed from the market. Korean companies will be competing against state-owned Chinese companies and mostly multinational local subsidies in an open Chinese market. China's companies also have to confront the challenges from strong, competitive Korea companies such as Samsung, LG, LK, and Hyundai so on.

To maximize the net effects of a CK-FTA, Korea and China should both accelerate vertical integration within industries to increase intra-industry trade. And restructuring of intra-industry divisions can help to avoid domestic deindustrialization. Also, it is necessary to consider the fact that such a policy causes domestic demand and exports to develop at the same time. Benefits from foreign policy can be achieved not by destroying the domestic industry, but by developing an industry for domestic demand.[73] The scenario choice will definitely cause different

<hr />

73) Hongshik Lee, Hyejoon Lm, Inkoo Lee, Backhoon Song, Soonchan Park, Seoul: KIEP, December 30, 2005.

effects for the two countries' economic indicators, which implies that the effects of CK-FTA are not fixed, but that they can be changed relying on how the two countries utilize the opportunities to melt into a more liberalized world markets together by maintaining specific cooperative strategies and policies for pursuing benefits. Therefore, it should be noted that the estimated effects of a CK-FTA only represent the potential gains. There are pros and cons to both sides at the same time.

Actually, it is impossible for all firms and industries to enjoy the FTA benefits, since both countries have their relative advantages and disadvantages varying from agriculture to manufacture, even in the service sectors. However, if the two countries could choose an appropriate scenario in a macroeconomic sense, C-K FTA's side effects would be alleviated for both countries. As the research shows, the total economic effect measured by GDP and welfare will offset the negative effects induced by this FTA.

02 | Policy Implications

The costs for not engaging in an FTA between Korea and China would be large, especially for Korea. Depending on two scenarios, Korea's welfare would both benefit greatly. The Chinese market is one of the world's largest markets, and China has now become Korea's biggest trade partner and biggest export market. If Korea gave up an FTA with China, potential economic and political gains would go into other countries' pockets. Other countries will seize upon good opportunity for growth while Korea hesitates. The opportunity cost may include losing gains from trade, losing investments and even losing efficiency. And so would China. Furthermore, an FTA would send a strong signal to world investors of a strengthened relationship, the value of which is difficult to estimate numerically. A possible CK-FTA would significantly contribute to deepening the economic relations and enhancing the intra-industry trade between China and Korea. If not for a CK-FTA, both countries' potential efficiency gains in all industries would get lost.

Two major policy implications can be derived from this research. First, according to the competitiveness analysis made in the thesis, China is more competitive in food, crude materials, and vegetables and so on, which are mostly labor-intensive industries. Compared to China, Korea is strongly competitive in relative capital-intensive industries like chemicals, machinery and transport equipment. Therefore, in the negotiation process, these sectors will probably become the bargaining focus or key point. In other words, China's relative competitive products will be sensitive in Korea's perspective, and vice versa. Before signing the FTA, much research should focus on the two sides' sensitive sectors. The Korean government should increase and balance its subsidies toward a reform that innovates and upgrades agricultural industries and make gradual and constructive process to help its farmers to face and adapt international market competition. And the agricultural reform measure, more importantly, would boost Korea's credibility in its ambition for taking a leading role toward the economic integration of the Northeast Asian region. So should China's reform measures for its manufactures.

Second, the two countries' FTA strategies have strong political motives. On the political side, China entered into a rivalry with Japan for leadership over the East-Asia region, with Japan attempting to control the rise of China. This is reflected by the fact that China is actively promoting economic cooperation with ASEAN and Korea in an attempt to hold back the rapid expansion of FTAs between Japan and other countries in the region. On the Korean side, for the time being, Korea has put FTAs with China and Japan aside in favor of actively pursuing FTAs with the USA, EU, and Australia. Considering the two countries' stance toward FTAs in a political-economic context, I suggest that both countries should actively pursue multi-track FTA talks with major existing trading partners until the CK-FTA has matured to emerge. Probably the CK-FTA will not be signed until Korea has achieved satisfaction with its global economic adjustment strategy. This means that Korea will prefer FTAs with USA, EU and some other non-Northeast Asian countries. From this point of view, CK-FTA strategies are competitive, to some degree. However, Korea has signed an FTA with the United States and is planning another one with the European Union. Thus for the moment, the worry of "if China sneezes, Korea will catch a cold" has been alleviated. Just as "A Korea-U.S. FTA would be able to function as a balance to decrease dependence on the Chinese economy and decrease the potential for dependency on any specific country,"[74] a coming CK-FTA, for Korea's balanced diplomatic policy, would also function as KORUS does.

---

74) Ibidem.

Acknowledgements

Research, analysis, and logistics for this dissertation project have been extensive and at times overwhelming, but in the end I can say this has been a highly stimulating, instructive, and enormously rewarding period of my life. This thesis is the result of three years of work during which I have been accompanied and supported by many people. It is now a pleasant task that I am in the position to express my gratitude to all of them.

First of all, I would like to thank Dr. Seok-Keun Park. Through his advice I received much encouragement and guidance to a deeper understanding of East Asian economic knowledge. His invaluable comments during the phase of my research have helped to shape my thinking about thesis topics in various ways.

I am eager to give special thanks to Professor Jong-Hwan Ko who helped me to put important last touches on this paper. I have known Professor Ko as a principled and highly structured economist who has experienced his field in many universities around the world. His insightful views on CGE model and his mission toward providing "only high-quality work and not less" have left a deep impression on me.

I also want to express my gratefulness to Professor Sang-Kuk Chung who provided me with much needed help not only toward my research but also about the well-being of my personal life. Besides being an excellent advisor, Professor Chung is also a good friend as close as a relative to me. I am really glad I came to know Professor Chung in this phase of my life. I also need to express my sincere thanks to Professor Kwang-Bong Lee and Professor Bong-Ho Choi who both cooperated well with me and who offered many proficient suggestions for this paper.

The dramatic conclusion of this thesis depended on help from an unexpected corner of trade economics, namely from Dr. Terrie L. Walmsley, Director and Research Assistant Professor in the GTAP Research Center at Purdue University, Indiana, USA. She has been very kind in helping me improve my GTAP analysis with discerning experience, although I am a stranger to her.

I would like to extent special thanks to my good friend Dr. Michael Reinschmidt, Visiting Professor of Korean Studies. Our mutual interests especially in Korea's farm-related FTA issues have been discussed intensely from the stimulating perspectives of cultural anthropology to help guide me through the maze of Korea's domestic and international agricultural relations.

Meanwhile, I am glad to come forth and express my sincere thankfulness to Professor Du-Su Choi, Professor Han-Gyoun Kang and all the other professors in our international business department. Their important courses benefited me much to acquire crucial knowledge in world and regional economics.

Finally, I am very grateful to my family, friends, and classmates, all of whom have tolerated, carried, and enjoyed me greatly during the years of my graduate work. Without their encouragement, support, and help I would never have been able to finish this project.

References

■ English:

A Report for the Department of Foreign Affairs and Trade by the Australian APEC Study Centre, Monash University August, 2001.

Akamatsu, Kaname. "A Historical Pattern of Economic Growth in Developing Countries," *The Developing Economies*, 1, March-August, 1962.

Alston, J. M., C. A. Carter, R. Green, and D. Pick. "Whither Armington Trade Models?" *American Journal of Agricultural Economics*, 1990, 72(2):455-467.

Anderson, K., J. Francois, T. Hertel, B. Hoekman and W. Martin. "Potential Gains from Trade Reform in the New Millennium." Centre for International Economic Studies, University of Adelaide, 2000.

Aquino, A. (1981). "Change over time in the pattern of comparative advantage in manufactured goods: An empirical analysis for the period 1972-1974," *European Economic Review*, 1981, 15: 41-62.

Argy, V., W. McKibbin, and E. Siegloff. "Exchange Rate Regimes for a Small Economy in a Multi-Country World," *Princeton Studies in International Economics, 1989, 67.*

Ariff, Mohamed. "Outlooks for ASEAN Externalities," In Shoji Nishijima, 1996..

Armington, P. A. "A Theory of Demand for Products Distinguished by Place of Production," *IMF Staff Papers*, 1969, 16:159-178.

ASEAN-China Expert Group. "Forging closer ASEAN-China Economic Relations in the 21 Century, A Report by the ASEAN-China Group on Economic Cooperation, October, 2001.

Balassa, Bela. "Trade Liberalization and 'Revealed' Comparative Advantage," *Manchester School*, 1965, 33: 99-123.

Balasubramanyam, V. N. and D. Greenaway. "Regional Integration Agreements and Foreign Direct Investmet," Chapter 7 in K. Anderson and R. Blackhurst (1993), 147-166

Baldwin, R. E. "The Growth Effects of 1992," *Economic Policy*, 1989, 4(9).

Baldwin, R. E. "Measurable Dynamic Gains from Trade." *Journal of Political Economy*, 1992, 100(1).

Baldwin, R.E. "A Domino Theory of Regionalism," *NBER Working Paper no.*

4465, National Bureau of Economic Research, Cambridge, MA, 1993.

Baldwin, Richard. "The Spoke Trap: hub and spoke bilateralism in East Asia," *KIEP CNAEC Research Series 04-02*, Korea Institute for International Economic Policy, 2004.

Bhagwati, Jagdish, David Greenaway, and Arvind Panagariya. "Trading preferentially: theory and policy", The Economic Journal, 1998, 108: 1128-1148.

Bhagwati, Jagdish. "U.S. Trade Policy: The Infatuation with Free Trade Areas" in Jagdish Bhagwati and Anne O. Krueger. The Dangerous Drift to Preferential Trade Agreements, *the AEI Press*, 1995: 1-18.

Bhagwati, Jagdish, Testimony, Subcommittee on Domestic and International Monetary Policy, Trade and Technology, U.S. House of Representatives, Tuesday, April 1, 2003.

Booz Allen Hamilton. Revitalizing the Korean Economy towards the 21st Century. Report for Vison Korea Committee. Booz-Allen-Hamilton Inc. October, 1997.

Bosello, F., and J. Zhang. "Assessing Climate Change Impacts: Agriculture," FEEM [Fondazione Eni Enrico Mattei], Working Paper 94, 2005.

Brockmeier, M. "A Graphical Exposition of the GTAP Model," GTAP Technical Paper, Center for Global Trade Analysis, Purdue University, West Lafayette, IN, 1996.

Chis Siow Yue. "Regional economic cooperation in East Asia: approaches and process," in "East Asian Cooperation: progress and future," *World Affairs Press*, 2003: 37.

Cho, Hyun-Jun. "China's Political Approach toward FTAs with East Asia Nations and Its Implications for Korea," *Journal of International Economic Studies*, 8(1), 2004.

Christine McDaniel, Alan Fox. "U.S.-Korea FTA: The Economic Impact of Establishing a Free Trade Agreement(FTA) Between the United States and the Republic of Korea," USITC, September, 2001.

Chun, Soo Bong, "Developing New Industries to Improve the Nation's Economic Competitiveness," *ITBI Review*, 19(2), December, 2003: 33-50.

Coyle, John. Rules of Origin as Instruments of Foreign Economic Policy: An Analysis of the Integrated Sourcing Initiative in the U.S.-Singapore Free Trade Agreement. *Yale Journal of International Law*, 2004, 24:545.

De Melo, Jaime, and Arvind Panagariya. "New regionalism," *Finance and Development*,

29 December, 1992.

DeRosa, D, and J.P. Gilbert. "Predicting Trade Expansion under FTAs and Multilateral Agreements," *Working paper WP05-13, Institute for International Economics*, October 2005.

Dimaranan, B.V., and R. McDougall, eds. Global Trade, Assistance, and Production: The GTAP 6 Data Base. West Lafayette, IN: Center for Global Trade Analysis, Purdue University, 2006.

Doroodian, K., R.G. Boyd, and M. Piracha. "A CGE Analysis of the Impact of Trade Liberalization between the United States and Mexico," *Atlantic Economic Journal*, 1994, 22, no. 4: 43 - 54.

Ethier, Wilfred J. "The New Regionalism", *the Economic Journal*, Vol 108, No 449, July, 1998.

Feldstein, M. "Domestic Savings and International Capital Movements in the Long Run and Short Run," *European Economic Review*, 1983, 21:129-151.

Fernandez, Raquel. "Returns to Regionalism: An Evaluation of Non-Traditional Gains from RTAS". *NBER Working Paper Series*, National Bureau of Economic Research 1050 Massachusetts Avenue Cambridge, MA 02138 March, 1997.

Gouranga Gopal Das, Soamiely Andriamananjara. "Hub-and-Spoke Free Trade Agreements in the Presence of Technology Spillover: An Application to the Western Hemisphere". Hanyang University, Ansan; World Bank, Washington, D, C, 2006.

Greenaway, D. (2000). "Multilateralism, Miniliteralism and Trade Expansion", In D. Das (ed.), Asian Exports. Oxford University Press, Oxford.

Harilal, K.N. and P.L. Beena. The WTO Agreement on Rules of Origin: Implications for South Asia. CDS Working Paper 353, December, 2003.

Harrison, W. J. and K. R. Pearson. "Computing Solutions for Large General Equilibrium Models Using GEMPACK," Impact Project Preliminary Working Paper, 1994, No. IP-64.

Hertel, T., D. Hummels, M. Ivanic, and R. Keeney. "How Confident Can We Be in CGE - Based Assessments of Free Trade Agreements?" GTAP Working Paper 26, 2004.

Hertel, T.W.. *Global Trade Analysis: Modeling and Applications.* NY: Cambridge University Press, 1997.

Hongshik Lee, Hyejoon Lm, Inkoo Lee, Backhoon Song, Soonchan Park (2005) "Economic Effects of a Korea-China FTA and Policy Implications". Published on December 30, 2005 by KIEP (Institute for International Economic Policy), South Korea.

Hufbauer, G.L., and Y. Wong. "Prospects for Regional Free Trade in Asia," *Working Paper WP05-12*, Institute for International Economics, October, 2005.

Ianchovichina, Elena and Robert McDougall. "Theoretical Structure of Dynamic GTAP," *GTAP Technical Paper No. 17*, Edition 1.1 Draft 9, December, 2000.

Ianchovichian, E., and T. Walmsley. "Impact of China's WTO Accession on East Asia," Working Paper, World Bank, 2003.

Jeffrey J. Schott. Institute for International Economics November 10, 2003.

Jomini, P., J.F. Zeitsch, R. McDougall, A. Welsh, S. Brown, J. Hambley, and J. Kelly. "SALTER: A General Equilibrium Model of the World Economy," 1991, Vol. 1, "Model Structure, Database and Parameters." Canberra, Australia: Industry Commission.

Joseph Alba, Jung Hur, and Donghyun Park. Do Hub-and-Spoke Free Trade Agreements Increase Trade? A Panel Data Analysis. ADB Working Paper Series on Regional Economic Integration. No. 46 | April 2010

Kim Joon-Kyung, Kim Yangseon and Chung H. Lee. "Trade and Investment between China and South Korea: Toward a Long-Term Partnership," *The Journal of the Korean Economy*, Vol. 5, No. 1 (Spring 2004), 97-124.

Kim, Joon-Kyung and Chung H. Lee. "Korea's Direct Investment in China and Its Implications for Economic Integration in Northeast Asia," *Journal of Economic Policy*, 25(2), 2003.

Korean Ministry of Foreign Affairs and Trade. Korea's FTA Policy, 2005.

Krishna, Pravin, "Regionalism and Multilateralism: A Political Economy Approach," *Quarterly Journal of Economics*, 1998, 113(1): 227-251.

Krueger, A. Foreign Trade Regimes and Economic Development. Cambridge, M.A, 1978.

Krugman, Paul R. "A model of Innovation, Technology Transfer, and the World Distribution of Income," *Journal of Political Economy*, 1979, vol, 87, no.21.

Krugman, Paul. "The Move toward Tree Trade Zones," in Philip King, ed.,

International Economics and International Economics Policy: A Reader (McGraw-Hill: New York), 1995: 163-186.

Lazaro, Dorothea C. and Erlinda M. Medalla, "Rules of Origin: Evolving Best Practices for RTAs/FTAs." *Philippine Institute for Developments Studies*, Discussion Paper Series, No 2006-01.

Laursen, Keld, "Revealed Comparative Advantage and the Alternatives as Measures of International Specialization", DRUID Working Paper, 1998, No. 98-30.

Laursen, Keld. DRUID/IKE-Group Aalborg University PhD Thesis, 1998.

Lee, J. W. "International Trade, Distortions, and Long-Run Economic Growth", *IMF Staff Papers 40*, 1993: 299-328.

Lee, J. W. "Capital Goods Imports and Long-Run Growth", *Journal of Development Economics* 48,1995: 91-110.

Levine, R. and D. Renelt. "A Sensitivity Analysis of Cross-Country Growth Regressions." *American Economic Review* 82, 1992: 942-963.

Lim, K.T (1997). "Analysis of North Korea's Foreign Trade by Revealed Comparative Advantage," *Journal of Economic Development*, Vol. 22, 1997: 97-117.

Long, Guoqiang and Liping Zhang. "China: From Open Regionalism to Institutional Regional Arrangement?" Presented at the KIEP's International Conference on Prospects for an East Asia FTA, Seoul. September, 2002.

Luca De Benedictis, Roberta De Santis and e Claudio Vicarelli. "Hub-and Spoke or else? Free trade agreements in the enlarged European Union", Presented at the Conference "The new frontiers of European Union" organized by CEPII, CEFI and *Revue Economique*, held in Marrakech the 16-17 March 2005.

Magee, Christopher, "New Measures of Trade Creation and Trade Diversion," mimeo, 2004.

Magee, Christopher. "Trade Creation, Trade Diversion, and Endogenous Regionalism", 2005.

http://www.facstaff.bucknell.edu/cmagee/Trade%20Creation,%20Trade%20Diversion%20and%20 20Endogenous%20Regionalism.pdf

Mallikamas, S. "A Study of Thailand's Readiness to Establish Free Trade Areas," working paper Chulalongkorn University, 2002.

Mundell, R. "Tariff Preferences and the Terms of Trade," *Manchester School of*

Economic and Social Studies, January, 1964: 1-13.

Ng, Francis and Alexander Yeats. "Major trade trends in East Asia", *World Bank Policy Research Working Paper 3084*, June, 2003.

Okamoto Jiro (ed.). Whither free trade arrangements? IDE, JETRO, Tokyo, 2003: 246.

Park Innwon. "East Asian Regional Trade Agreements: Do They Promote Global Free Trade?" *Korea and the World Economy, V: Korea and the FTA*, July 8-8, 2006, Korea University, Seoul, Korea.

Parthasarathy, G. "India and Free Trade in Asia," *Business line* (Chennai) June, 2006, 16: 1. *MARCH - APRIL 2007 35.*

Rahul Sen. Free Trade Agreements in Southeast Asia (Singapore: Institute of Southeast Asian Studies), 2004: 75-84.

Razeen, Sally. "China's Trade Policies and its Integration into the World Economy." Paper prepared for the IGD/SAIIA SACU-China FTA Workshop, Johannesburg, September, 2004: 28-29.

Ravenhill, John and Yang Jiang. "China's Move to Preferential Trading: An Extension of Chinese Network Power?" paper presented at the International Conference "Made in China vs. Made by Chinese: Global Identities of Chinese Business", Collingwood College, Durham University, Durham, United Kingdom, March, 2007: 19-20.

Rieder, Roland. "Playing Dominoes in Europe: An Empirical Analysis of the Domino Theory for the EU, 1962-2004." HEI Working Paper, No: 11/2006.

Richardson, David J., Revealing Comparative Advantage: Chaotic or Coherent Patterns across Time and Sector and US Trading Partner, NBER Working Papers, w7212.

Sachs, J. D. and A. Warner. "Economic Reform and the Process of Global Integration", Brookings Papers on Economic Activity 1, 1995, pp. 1-118.

Schiff, M., and L. A. Winters. "Regional Integration as Diplomacy", *The World Bank Economic Review,* May 1988, Vol. 12, No. 2: 271-295.

Schiff, Maurice and L. Alan Winters. "Regional Integration and Development: Implications from World Bank Research for ACP and Latin American Countries", *The Journal of World Trade*. June 2002 (with L.Alan Winters) - Abstracted in CSA Worldwide Political Science Abstract.

Siegfried Bender. Trade and Comparative advantage of Asia and Latin American

Manufactured Export, APEC study center consortium conference, 2001.

Suranovic, Steven (1997-2004). "Trade Diversion and Trade Creation", *The South Korean Yonhap News Agency*, 2005.

The Joint Study Report for China-Korea FTA. The Joint Study Committee has held 5 meetings for the period from March 2007 and to May 2010. The Group reaffirms that the content and scope of this report is without prejudice to the future positions of each government in the negotiations for a possible China-Korea FTA.

Toranomon Kaikan. "China's Full Market Economy: ASEAN", *Straits Times*, September 7, 2004.

Viner, Jacob. *The Customs Union Issue*, Carnegie Endowment for International Peace: New York, 1950.

Waldkirch. Andreas, "The 'New Regionalism' and Foreign Direct Investment: The Case of Mexico," *Journal of International Trade and Economic Development*, June, 2003, 12(2): 151-184.

Warren, T. "The Impact on Output of Impediment to Trade and Investment in Telecommunications Services", In C. Findlay and T, 2001.

Warren eds. *Impediments to Trade in Services: Measurement and Policy Implications*. Routledge: London and New York.

Whalley, John. "Why Do Countries Seek Regional Trade agreements?"In Frankel, Jeffrey A. ed, *The Regionalization of the World Economy, The University of Chicago Press*, 1989: 71-72.

Winters, L. A. "Separability and the Specification of Foreign Trade Functions," *Journal of International Economics* 17: 239-241, 1984.

Wonnacott and Lutz. "Is There a Case for Free Trade Agreements?" in Schott, J., ed., *Free Trade Areas and U.S. Trade Policy* (Institute for International Economics: Washington D.C.) 1989: 59-84.

World Bank, Trade Blocs: A World Bank Policy Research Report. *Oxford University Press*, 2002.

WTO, "Rules of Origin Regimes in Regional Trade Agreements," Background Survey by the Secretariat. WT/REB/W/45. April 5, 2002.

WTO, "The Changing Landscape of RTAs," Seminar on RTA and the WTO. WTO, Secretariat, Geneva 14, November, 2003.

Xiaming Liu and David Parker. "Changes in China Comparative Advantage in

Manufacturing 1987-95: A Statistical Study," Aston Business School Research Paper (6), 2000.

Yeyati, Eduardo Levy, Ernesto Stein, and Christian Daude. "Regional Integration and the Location of FDI," Working Paper No. 492. Inter-American Development Bank, 2003.

Yoriko Kawaguchi's policy speech. "Building bridges toward our future: Initiating for reinforcing SEAN integration", June 17, 2003.

Zhao Jianping. "FTA The new approach for China's FTA cooperation, China' State Council Research Centre, investigation research report No.76, Total No.1925"

Zhang Jianping. "Analysis on the Issues of and Prospects for a China-Korea FTA" KIEP CNAEC Research Series 06-04, Published November 30, 2006 in Korea by KIEP

■ Chinese:

程恩富, 夏晖, "东亚经济的调整与合作", ≪财经研究≫, 2003, (7).

冯昭奎, 10+3：走向东亚自由贸易区之路, ≪世界经济与政治≫, 2002, (3).

谷克鉴, 吴宏, 外向型贸易转移: 中国外贸发展模式的理论验证与预期应用. 管理世界, 2003, (6).

郭继丰, "中国FTA战略: 合作供赢全球均衡", 上海社科院.

胡鞍钢, "建立三国四方自由贸易区设想", ≪国际经济评论≫, 2001, (2).

姜丁实, "东亚制造业分工现状及韩国的建议". 韩国对外经济政策研究院, 2005年1月.

柳宽容, "中日韩对各产业的影响及可行性分析", 产业研究院, 2004年12月.

强永昌, "产业内贸易论－－国际贸易最新理论, "复旦大学出版社, (2002).

唐朱昌, 毛作文, "东亚经济合作方式及其对中国的利益－基于历史经验的模型分析", ≪世界经济研究≫2005年第11期

田中青："东亚合作与中国的战略利益", ≪当代亚太≫2003年第5期.

王国安, 范昌子, "中欧贸易互补性研究－基于比较优势理论和产业内贸易理论的实证分析".

徐奇渊 刘力臻, "中国参与国际区域一体化: 文献综述" 东北师范大学.

薛敬孝,张伯伟, "东亚经济合作安排", ≪世界经济≫, 2004, (6).

张慧智, "中日韩FTA对产业的影响分析", ≪东北亚论坛≫, 2006年7月 (4).

张琦 吕 刚, "如何对待敏感产业: 中国已签署自贸区协议对中日韩FTA的
　　启示", 国务院发展研究中心 "中日韩自贸区影响研究"课题组. 张曙
　　宵, "中国对外贸易结构论," 中国经济出版社, (2003).
张蕴岭, "东亚合作与中国----东盟自由贸易区的建设", ≪当代亚太≫, 2002, (3).
赵晋平, "FTA我国参与区域经济合作的新途径", 中国国务院研究中心, 调查研
　　究报告, 第76号, 总1925号, 2003年7月.

■ Korean:

김준동 외. 2008.「서비스협상의 Mode 4 관련 대응방안 연구: 독립전문
　　가를 중심으로」, 대외경제정책연구원·한국노동연구원.
김양희. 2010.「일본의 '포괄적 EPA 기본방침'에 대한 평가와 시사점」.
　　대외경제정책연구원.
김한성 외. 2008.「한국FTA 원산지규정의 특성 및 활용전략」. 대외경제
　　정책연구원. 남풍우.
안재진. 2007.「EU와의 FTA 체결협상에 따른 범유럽 원산지규정 운용의
　　특징 분석과대응방안 연구」.『무역학회지』, 제32권 제4호, pp.
　　1~24. 한국무역학회.
유길상 외. 2004.「WTO 서비스 협상 관련 각국의 노동시장 개방현황 및
　　정책과제 연구」 노동부.
이규용 허재준. 2008.「이민정책의 환경변화와 아태지역 인력이동 협력
　　을 위한 정책과제」. 한국노동연구원.
이장규 외. 2008.「한중 FTA 대비 중국의 FTA 서비스협정 분석과 정책
　　제언」. 대외경제정책연구원.
이창수. 2008.「지역통합의 무역전환효과: 동아시아와 미주지역 비교」.
　　『응용경제』, 제10권 제1호. 한국응용경제학회.
이창재 외. 2009.「동아시아 FTA 실현을 위한 당면과제와 해결방안」. 대
　　외경제정책연구원. 2005.『한중일 FTA의 경제적 파급효과 및 대응
　　전략』. 대외경제정책연구원.
허재준·이규용·박성재. 2008.「통상협상에서의 전문직 인력이동 관련 대
　　응방안」. 노동부,『중국의 기체결 FTA 협정문』(중-홍콩 CEPA, CNZFTA,
　　중-칠레 FTA, 중-싱가포르FTA 등).
방호경. 2008.「동아시아 지역의 산업별 생산분할 특징과 시사점」. 대외
　　경제정책연구원.

정인교 외. 2005.『우리나라 FTA 원산지규정 연구 및 실증분석』. 한국경
    제연구원.
정재화. 2009.「동아시아 FTA의 경제적 효과와 추진전략」. 한남대학교
    대학원 박사학위논문.
최낙균 외. 2008.『한·중·일 3국의 FTA 비교분석과 동북아 역내국간
    FTA 추진방향』. 대외경제정책연구원.
최은정.「FTA 원산지규정 관련 간담회 자료」. 대외경제정책연구원.

■ Website:

http://www.apec.org/
http://www.apectariff.org/
http://www.app.fta.gov.sg/
http://www.aseansec.org/
http://www.bea.gov/
http://www.bilaterals.org/
http://www.bok.or.kr/eng/index.jsp
http://www.census.gov/
http://www.chinadaily.com.cn/english/
http://www.china.org.cn/
http://comtrade.un.org/
http://www.cqvip.com/
http://www.customs.gov.cn/
http://www.ebscohost.com/
http://www.fao.org/statistics/
http://www.fta.go.kr
http://www.fx.sauder.ubc.ca/data.html
http://www.gjs.mofcom.gov.cn
http://www.global.kita.net/
http://www.gmxh.mofcom.gov.cn/
http://goliath.ecnext.com/
http://www.gtap.agecon.purdue.edu/
http://www.imf.org/
http://www.kiep.go.kr/eng/

http://www.koreaexim.go.kr/
http://www.kosis.kr/
http://www.kr.mofcom.gov.cn/
http://www.mofa.go.jp/
http://www.mofat.go.kr/
http://www.mofcom.gov.cn/
http://www.news.bbc.co.uk/
http://www.news.xinhuanet.com/english/
http://www.oecd.org/
http://www.singtaonet.com
http://www.stats.gov.cn/
http://www.stats.unctad.org/
http://www.tid.gov.hk/english/
http://www.un.org
http://www.unstats.un.org/
http://www.ustr.gov/
http://www.uwashington.worldcat.org/
http://www.wits.worldbank.org
http://www.worldbank.org/
http://www.wto.org/

Appendix 1

VOA: Value of output at agent's price

PTX: Producer tax/subsidy

VOM: Value of output at market price

VXMD: Value of exports at market price by Destination

VST: Value of sales to transport

VDM: Value of domestic sales at market price

XTAXD: Export tax/subsidy by destination

VXWD: Value of exports at world price by destination

VTWR: Value of transport at world price by route

VIWS: Value of imports at world price by source

MTAX: Import taxes by source

VIMS: Value of imports by source at market price

VIM: Value of aggregate imports at market price

VIPM: Value of imports by private household at market price

VIGM: Value of imports by government at market price

VIFM: Value of imports by firms at market price

Appendix 2

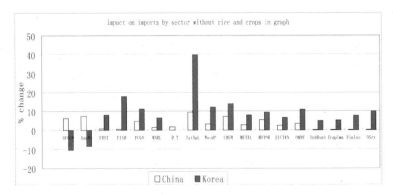

Source: made by author. Note (the sector figures exclude rice and crops)

Figure V-(7-1) Effects on Korea and China's Imports by Sectors in Full Scenario

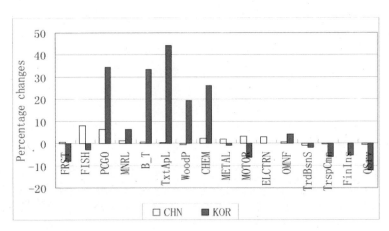

Source: made by author. Note (the sector figures exclude "rice", "crops", "other food products" and "animals and meat")

Figure V-(8-1) Effects on Korea and China's Exports by Sectors in Full Scenario

The Feasibility of a Korea-China FTA and its Potential Economic Effects

Doctor Zhao Jin long received his Ph.D at INJE University of South Korea. He is currently an Assistant Professor of School of Economics at Shanghai University. He got more that ten years teaching experience and has more than 5 years corporate and consultancy experience.

Academic and Professional Qualification

2005.9 ~ 2008.6 Doctor Course Study of International Business at INJEUniversity, SouthKorea.
2004.9 ~ 2005.7 Master Course Study of International Business at INJEUniversity, SouthKorea.
2002.9 ~ 2004.7 Master Course Study of International Law of Qingdao University, China.

Biography

Doctor Zhao has an excellent education background in International Economics and Business, being familiar with theory of International Economic Integration and Trade Policies. He has a very solid ability to providing personnel and organizational management and accomplishing training objectives with good experiences in personnel managements and organization with providing leadership and support.

Teaching and Professional Experience

Courses taught:

Oct 2008 ~ Current   Shanghai University, China

MBA Program

- Executive Economics

  Graduate Courses

- Advanced International Trade Theory
- International Trade Theory and Policy

  Undergraduate Courses

- Modern Economics
- China's Foreign Trade
- Macroeconomics
- Microeconomics
- WTO and China
- International Economic Cooperation

Working Experience

Economics, at Shanghai University of China

- 2006.4 ~ 2008.6 Training supervisor in Career Development Center of INJE University, Republic of Korea
- 2006.9 ~ 2008.6 Work as a senior trainer responsible for providing support to new trainees through mentoring, observation, and feedback for Shandong "ChengWang" Companyand Shandong "JianKai" Company and made great achievements
- 2005.9 ~ 2008.6 Perform as a senior counselor of China's Market and responsible for the market development of Korean P&H International Trade Company
- 2004.9 ~ 2005.12 Researcher of BK21 Program of Ministry of Education and Human Resources Development, South Korea
- 2002.10 ~ 2004.6 English and Law Training Lecturer in Adult Education Institute of Qingdao University

Publications

Articles

- "South Korea-EU FTA's Impact on China's Foreign Trade", **Northeast forum**, No.4, 2011. CSSCI Journal.
- "South Korea's FTA Strategy and its Motives", **Korea Research**, Fudan University, No.19, 3, 2011.
- "South Korea-USA FTA's impact on China's Foreign Trade", **International Business**, No.3, 2009, CSSCI.
- "The Economic Effects and Prediction of China-Korea FTA", **Korea Research**, Fudan University. No.19, 2, 2008.
- "The Direction of China's FTA Strategy in Northeast Asia: a Comparative Research of CGE Model", *Northeast Forum*, No.4, 2008.
- "The Potential Economic Effects of China-Korea FTA: GTAP Analysis", *Korean Tradeand Commerce*, Volume7, No.4, December, 2007, pp.47-77.
- "An Analysis of Trade Competitiveness and Complementarities between Korea and China", *Korean Trade and Commerce*, Volume7, No.1, March, 2007, pp.3-27.
- "A Comparative Research between Korea and China's FTA Strategies", *Korean Tradeand Commerce*, Volume 6, No.2, December, 2006, pp.111-142.
- "Theoretical Analysis and Effect of Green barrier on International Agric-product Trade of China", *Journal of University of Electronic Science and Technology of China(Social Sciences Edition)*, No.5, 2006.
- "On Theoretical Analysis of SPS and International Agric-prod Trade in Post-transition Period", *Business Research*, No.23, 2006.

The Feasibility of a Korea-China FTA and its Potential Economic Effects

한국-중국의 실현 가능한
FTA와 잠재적 경제효과

초 판 인 쇄 | 2012년 12월 6일
초 판 발 행 | 2012년 12월 6일

지 은 이 | Zhao Jin long
펴 낸 이 | 채종준
펴 낸 곳 | 한국학술정보㈜
주   소 | 경기도 파주시 문발동 파주출판문화정보산업단지 513-5
전   화 | 031) 908-3181(대표)
팩   스 | 031) 908-3189
홈 페 이 지 | http://ebook.kstudy.com
E-mail | 출판사업부 publish@kstudy.com
등   록 | 제일산-115호(2000. 6. 19)

ISBN   978-89-268-3893-8-93340 (Paper Book)
         978-89-268-3894-5-95340 (e-Book)

 한국학술정보㈜의 학술 분야 출판 브랜드입니다.